Carole Sobell's

NEW
Jewish
CUISINE

Carole Sobell's
NEW *Jewish* CUISINE

PHOTOGRAPHY BY LAURIE EVANS

· K·U·P·E·R·A·R·D ·

I would like to give a special thank you to
my Mum and Ernie for all their love, guidance and support;
to Sylvia and Harold Sobell for everything they taught me;
and to my children, Bianca and Jonathan, for their patience
and who mean the world to me. Another special thank you
to Hilary and Cyril Dennis, Andrea, Victoria and Jonathan
for their continued family friendship and support.

Photographer: Laurie Evans

Stylist: Lesley Richardson

Photographic assistant: Andy Grimshaw

Designer: Robert Kelland

Editor: Phil McNeill

With thanks to Rachel Bentham, Juliette Ellis, Rick Fowden,
Judith Hannam, Dawn Kohn, Clair Reynolds, Caroline Warde,
to Jake Watkins for his outstanding culinary expertise in the line of fire,
and to Lara Piercy and Rob Brown at Colour Systems

My special thanks to Scott MacRae, whose advice and patience were invaluable

First published in Great Britain in 2001 by Kuperard
311 Ballards Lane, London N12 8LY

publications@kuperard.co.uk

Text copyright © Kuperard

Kuperard is an imprint of Bravo Ltd

A catalogue record for this title is available from the British Library

ISBN 1857332946

Production by Mike Powell & Associates (01494 676891)
Origination by Colour Systems Ltd, London
Printed and bound in Italy by Giunti Industrie Grafiche

Contents

6

NEW JEWISH CUISINE

hat exactly makes a dish 'Jewish'? So many diverse cultures have had an influence on our food over the years that it is now truly international. Jewish communities scattered across the globe have all brought their own distinctive local elements to bear. Today, recipes which can trace their origins back to biblical times sit comfortably alongside more modern offerings.

Contemporary Jewish food is a truly cosmopolitan mix – and Carole Sobell, as a leading Jewish caterer, has taken that one step further by integrating the best of the world's cuisines into the food she presents to her guests. Now, when Carole draws up a menu for a banquet, the only question that really matters is: "Is it kosher?"

The Hebrew word kosher literally means 'fit'. The religious laws of kashrut lay down strict rules to ensure that food is 'fit' for the Jewish table. Meat must come only from animals that have a split hoof and chew the cud, which allows for cattle, sheep and goats for example but excludes pigs, as well as horses and camels. To be kosher, meat or fowl must only come from ritually slaughtered animals and must be salted, soaked or broiled to remove the blood, as it is strictly forbidden to eat it. Fish must have fins and scales – which excludes all shellfish. The Bible also contains a precise list of non-kosher fowl, which includes birds of prey.

In culinary terms, one of the most restrictive rules is the separation of milk and meat, which must not be cooked or served together in the same meal. The rule can be traced to the biblical command "You shall not boil a kid in its mother's milk", which was translated to mean that meat and dairy must be kept separate.

Readers from more orthodox communities will automatically recognise the practical translation of this law. At home, you will use separate cooking dishes and utensils for milk and meat dishes. You may even have entirely separate milk and meat sinks, and food storage and preparation areas. Your favourite Jewish restaurants may have completely separate milk and meat kitchens, or you may prefer to choose between dairy and meat restaurants when dining out.

For a kosher catering company such as Carole Sobell's, obtaining the necessary licence from the rabbinical authorities is very exacting, and non-Jews often find the restrictions bewildering. "You mean you follow all these complicated rules – and still manage to produce delicious food!" It's a bit like asking a champion boxer to fight with one hand tied behind his back, and is not the kind of thing your average temperamental chef has to deal with…

The most notable difference, in practical terms, between a Jewish and non-Jewish caterer's kitchen is the presence of the shomer – a person trained in the laws of kashrut – who has to be on the premises during any food preparation to check and authorise each stage, from lighting the ovens to serving the food.

Koshering a kitchen which is to be used for food preparation at an outside venue takes around three hours. The ovens are 'burnt out' for at least an hour to rid them of any food particles, and the caterers will then install their own oven racks, or fix chicken wire to existing racks so that food does not come into contact with surfaces which may have been previously used to cook non-kosher foods.

In addition, all work surfaces are covered in foil, and dairy and meat products strictly separated.

Great care is taken to ensure the use of correct cooking utensils, which are labelled with blue tape for dairy and red for meat. A wrongly labelled utensil which has been left in the kitchen during any stage of preparing either

7

Carole Sobell's

meat or dairy dishes is quickly confiscated by the shomer, who has the authority to stop an event going ahead at any stage if he is not satisfied that every aspect of Jewish dietary law is fully met.

Any food which is to be served must pass the watchful eye of the shomer before it leaves the kitchens. All produce is thoroughly inspected. Salad leaves and green vegetables are shaken and examined against sheets of white paper for any sign of insects, whose consumption is strictly forbidden under Jewish law.

Wine and drinks to be served at the bar must also be 100 per cent kosher. For wine to be kosher, it must have a rabbinical seal of approval, which is given only to wines whose production has been supervised by that authority right from growing the grapes to bottling the finished product.

Certifying kosher wines is a complex business which has its roots in ancient Talmudic law. The law stated that it was strictly forbidden for Jews to drink wine which had been used for worshipping idols. Eventually this law encompassed all wines which had even been touched by Gentiles (non-Jews).

To many Jews, following the dietary laws is second nature, and cooks throughout the generations have experimented and adapted local recipes to suit their demands. For others, however, including those readers simply interested in adding a colourful new strand to their repertoire of recipes, these rules and restrictions may seem a little daunting.

Dinner invitations and menu planning can cause a headache for the host who is struggling to get to grips with a mix of guests, some of whom keep kosher, while others do not. Add a couple of vegetarians, an allergy sufferer and a guest requiring a low-cholesterol diet, and the only recipe facing the well-intentioned host could be one for disaster! It's worth making sure you know the dietary habits and needs of all your guests, including the question of whether they will only drink kosher wines, before you start planning your dinner party.

As for the rest of the menu, *Carole Sobell's New Jewish Cuisine* aims to simplify the matter by offering only dairy-free dishes which can therefore be served with meat or fish meals. They are also a source of inspiration for those avoiding dairy foods for health reasons alone.

This book does not seek to give an exhaustive explanation of the laws of kashrut, its historical origins and application in the home. Much has already been written on the subject to satisfy those interested in learning more. What it can do is reassure the observant that these tried and tested recipes are kosher, and where necessary have been carefully adapted to suit Jewish law while retaining their full flavours, tastes and textures.

8

9

10

NEW JEWISH CUISINE

Introduction • 'A bit of a do...'

The act of offering hospitality is regarded as a 'mitzvah', or good deed – and it is that desire to please and delight others which is the inspiration for *Carole Sobell's New Jewish Cuisine*. This book will help you to entertain your guests with style, whether it's a simple snack of salt beef sandwiches or a special occasion dinner.

Drawing on her 20 years' experience in catering, Carole has compiled a unique collection of recipes ranging from French-inspired fine dining to robust traditional rustic meals and deliciously different desserts that you will want to cook again and again. Among the collection are some favourites which have been served to the many people who turn to Carole Sobell's successful London-based catering business for major celebrations such as weddings, barmitzvahs and anniversary parties. Many of Carole's events celebrate those 'once-in-a-lifetime' moments for her clients, and their importance is reflected in the imagination and attention to detail which go into every one.

Few of us who set out to entertain are faced with the task of transporting a full-sized funfair complete with coconut shy, rifle range, bumper cars and a sawdust-strewn floor into a five-star hotel...

Carole's dramatic creations have included a tropical jungle in a hotel ballroom, lavish marquees with star-studded ceilings, and a riverside party where each guest setting came with its own live goldfish!

Yet even the professionals have to handle those moments when something doesn't go to plan. That's when

Scenes from a wedding: Carole talking canapés with her executive chef, Scott MacRae; with bride Lauren Rosenthal, who married Darren Tish in March 2000; and with Dorchester Hotel toastmaster David Collins, at the reception which Carole organised

Carole Sobell's

· Glossary ·

Agar-agar Gelatin substitute, made from seaweed

Assiette An assortment

Bake blind Baking pastry on its own to form a pastry case – see page 151

Baking parchment Non-inflammable greaseproof paper on which food is placed for baking

Balsamic A dark Italian vinegar with a sweet taste

Bird's-eye chillis Small hot red chillis

Blanch Boil vegetables and cool rapidly

Blow torch Obtainable at cookshops

Bok choi Chinese cabbage, also known as pak choi

Brisket Beef from the breast of the cow

Chargrill Cook quickly under a very hot grill or in a griddle pan

Court bouillon Wine and vegetable stock used in fish dishes

Crème anglaise Custard

Crêpe A thin pancake

Croûtons Cubes of fried, roasted or toasted bread

Crudités Raw vegetables, usually eaten with a dip

Dijon mustard Mild mustard from Dijon in Burgundy, France

Dredger Large sugar shaker

Duck confit Duck cooked slowly in its own fat

Duxelles Sauce or stuffing made from mushrooms and shallots

Fish kettle Pan for boiling fish

Flambé Set alight by igniting spirits to remove the alcohol

Gravadlax Dry-cured salmon – a dish of Scandinavian origin, also known as gravlax

Griddle Pan for chargrilling on a stove with ridges to give a striped effect

Latkes Grated potato pancakes

Lockshen Jewish noodles (vermicelli)

Mevushal Pasteurised

Nage Vegetable stock

Noisette A small, round piece of lamb or other meat

Nori Dried Japanese seaweed sheets used in sushi

Palmier A sweet pastry (originally they were shaped like palm leaves)

Pan-fry Fry in shallow oil, usually at high temperature

Parmentier potatoes Square, fried and roasted potatoes

Pesto An Italian sauce of basil, garlic and pine nuts, served with pasta or salads

Petit fours Tiny cakes or biscuits, highly decorative

Rack of lamb The front ribs

Ramekin Small dish for baking individual portions, usually ceramic

Reduce Boil to reduce in volume, thus thickening and/or intensifying the flavour

Rosti Grated potato, pan-fried and roasted

Simmer Keep on a low boil

Skim Take the fat off the top of a stock

Sorbet Water ice

Sushi A Japanese hors d'oeuvre consisting of rice and a filling in a roll or ball

Sweat Cook vegetables slowly in a little oil, bringing out their juices, with or without colour

Tapenade A Provençal dip made from black olives, anchovies and capers

Tartare sauce Mayonnaise mixed with gherkins and capers, which usually accompanies fish

Teriyaki A sweet soya sauce

Truffle *(savoury)* Strong-smelling fungus that grows underground

Truffle *(sweet)* A round chocolate-and-rum petit four

Tsimmes A classic Jewish stew

Tuile Curved biscuit

Velouté Sauce made from flour, margarine, cream substitute and stock

Wasabi Japanese mustard

12

13

Almost too good to eat... Carole puts the finishing touches to a tray of exquisitely-presented savoury tartlets

a party organiser's greatest asset is her sense of humour... Carole laughs as she remembers one particular party when thousands of scented rose petals fell romantically from the ceiling – and promptly turned the dance floor into a skating rink. Not wishing to interrupt the dance, out came a broom which became the partner for a tango which soon cleared the petals without anyone putting a foot wrong.

No effort is spared, whether Carole is catering for a client's party or entertaining her own friends and family at home. A self-confessed chocolate lover, she likes nothing

better than treating her guests to a selection of amazing desserts or trays of mouth-watering canapés, all beautifully presented – and many of her favourites are included in this book for you to create at home.

Larger, stage-managed events have to be run like a military operation with Carole, front of house, linked by walkie-talkie to her key staff in the kitchens and at the tables. It may be organised bedlam behind the scenes, but she ensures that the show runs smoothly, leaving the party host and guests to have a great time. And if you stick to the

Carole Sobell's

Shaken but not stirred... Carole loves to highlight her dishes with a dusting of caster sugar or a drizzle of coulis

same careful planning, it should guarantee successful entertaining at home – walkie-talkies optional!

As Carole says, it doesn't matter whether the dinner you are creating is for two or two hundred, you can make it happen, and make it memorable for all the right reasons. With a little forethought about setting the scene and presenting the food well, it need not be too difficult to make a lasting impression.

Carole Sobell's New Jewish Cuisine, with its tried-and-tested recipes presented in a modern restaurant style, is designed to help you dazzle.

Responding to the trend towards eating out more, fuelled by foreign travel and a more knowledgeable and sophisticated consumer, the recipes are drawn from a wide variety of culinary styles and cultures.

Carole's love of experimenting with new ways to

Carole Sobell's

NEW JEWISH CUISINE

Don't forget to leave room for the plates!

· Conversions ·

OVEN TEMPERATURES

Celsius	Fahrenheit	Gas
110	225	mark $^1/_4$
130	250	mark $^1/_2$
140	275	mark 1
150	300	mark 2
170	325	mark 3
180	350	mark 4
190	375	mark 5
200	400	mark 6
220	425	mark 7
230	450	mark 8

For fan-assisted ovens,
reduce temperatures by 10%

VOLUME

1.25ml		$^1/_4$ tsp
2.5ml		$^1/_2$ tsp
5ml		1 level tsp
15ml		1 level tbsp
30ml	1 fl oz	
50ml	2 fl oz	
150ml	5 fl oz	$^1/_4$ pint
200ml	7 fl oz	$^1/_3$ pint
300ml	10 fl oz	$^1/_2$ pint
425ml	15 fl oz	$^3/_4$ pint
600ml	20 fl oz	1 pint
700ml		$1^1/_4$ pints
850ml		$1^1/_2$ pints
1 litre		$1^3/_4$ pints
1.2 litres		2 pints
2 litres		$3^1/_2$ pints

WEIGHT

Grams	Ounces
10g	$^1/_2$ oz
20g	$^3/_4$ oz
25g	1 oz
50g	2 oz
75g	3 oz
110g	4 oz
150g	5 oz
175g	6 oz
200g	7 oz
225g	8 oz
250g	9 oz
275g	$9^1/_2$ oz
300g	$10^1/_2$ oz
350g	12 oz
375g	13 oz
400g	14 oz
425g	15 oz
450g	1 lb
700g	$1^1/_2$ lb
750g	1 lb 10 oz
1kg	$2^1/_4$ lb
1.25kg	2 lb 12 oz
1.5kg	3 lb 5 oz
2kg	$4^1/_2$ lb
2.25kg	5 lb
2.5kg	5 lb 8 oz
3kg	6 lb 8 oz

present food began in her late teens, when she would prepare the family's evening meal and hope to surprise them with what was on offer. Among this collection, therefore, you will find that many classic Jewish dishes such as smoked salmon have been given a new twist, as in the Assiette of Salmon – Teriyaki, Smoked and Gravadlax – with Oriental Salad. Elsewhere, modern-day classics such as Seared Tuna with Roquette and a Lime and Ginger Dressing, and Far Eastern dishes such as Thai Chicken Curry with Basmati Rice, sit alongside traditional comfort-food fillers such as Lancashire Hotpot.

All the recipes are kosher and dairy-free, and allow the reader to plan and serve exciting meals for any occasion with confidence. *Carole Sobell's New Jewish Cuisine* should help you to create your own special occasions – and share in Carole's love of 'making it happen'.

Carole Sobell's

Canapés

Smoked Salmon Mousse

Base recipe

150g / 5½ oz smoked salmon
50ml / 3 tablespoons cold vegetable stock (see page 79)
4 tablespoons mayonnaise
juice of ½ lemon
freshly ground black pepper

Blend all the ingredients until smooth, then chill.

Smoked Salmon Parcels

Makes 20 parcels

1 x Smoked Salmon Mousse recipe (see above)
20 x 5cm / 2-inch squares smoked salmon
1 bunch chives, blanched in boiling salted water

Put a teaspoon of mousse in the centre of each smoked salmon square. Tie as a money bag with a blanched chive.

Smoked Salmon Roulades

Makes 20 - 25 roulades

1 x Smoked Salmon Mousse recipe (see above)
4 slices smoked salmon

Lay the smoked salmon on a sheet of cling film. Smooth the mousse over it and roll like a roulade. Chill for 2 hours. Slice into small discs and place on toasted croûtons (see page 37) or on chunky sliced cucumber.

Smoked Salmon Rosettes

Makes 20 rosettes

20 ribbons smoked salmon (approx 300g in total)
20 discs toasted white, rye or pumpernickel bread
1 bunch chives, chopped
freshly ground black pepper

Roll the salmon ribbons into flower shapes – the easiest way to do this is with a pastry cutter. Place on the bread. Garnish with the chives and season with pepper.

Salmon in Filo

Makes 20

100g / 3½ oz cooked salmon
100g / 3½ oz smoked salmon, diced
50g / 1¾ oz tomato, skinned, de-seeded and diced
50g / 1¾ oz red pepper, diced
salt and freshly ground black pepper
1 bunch chives, chopped
1 packet filo pastry
olive oil

Preheat the oven to 190C / Gas 5.

Mix together the salmon, smoked salmon, tomato and red pepper, and season with salt and pepper and chopped chives.

Brush two sheets of filo with olive oil then cut into 3cm / 1⅓-inch squares. Place a teaspoon of the salmon mixture in the centre of each square and shape as a parcel.

On a baking tray, place the parcels on baking parchment or greaseproof paper and bake for 4-5 minutes until golden. Serve warm.

18

Carole Sobell's

Gravadlax with Dill Blinis

M a k e s   1 2

1 x 1kg / 2¼ lb side of salmon, skin on
1kg / 2¼ lb flaked sea salt
250g / 9 oz caster sugar
zest of a lemon
zest of a lime
2 bunches dill, finely chopped
20ml / ¾ oz mayonnaise

Mix the salt and sugar with the lemon and lime zest and juice. Line a plastic tray with cling film, then cover with half the salt mixture. Lay the salmon, skin side down, on top, and sprinkle with the dill. Cover with the remaining salt mixture.

Wrap the cling film tightly around the salmon, using more if necessary. Put another plastic tray on top, weight with something heavy, put in the refrigerator and leave for 24 hours, turning every 6 hours or so.

Scrape off any remaining salt and sugar, and slice very thinly. This will keep for a week.

BLINIS – FOR THE LEAVENING
15g / ½ oz yeast
250ml / 8 fl oz lukewarm soya milk
25g / 1 oz plain flour

≈

BLINIS – FOR THE BATTER
125g / 4½ oz buckwheat flour
2 eggs, separated
salt

Whisk together the leavening ingredients and leave in a warm place for 2 hours. Then mix the buckwheat flour and egg yolks into leavening mixture and leave for 1 hour.

Whisk the egg whites with a pinch of salt until stiff peaks form, then fold into the flour mixture.

Heat a large frying pan, brushed with a little oil, then pour a small teaspoon of batter into the centre and fry each side for 90 seconds. Drain on kitchen paper and cool. Continue until all the batter has been used.

Spread mayonnaise lightly on the blinis and place fine slices of gravadlax on top. Garnish with freshly-picked dill.

❋ Blinis can be made larger and used as a breakfast dish, under scrambled eggs, as an alternative to bagels.

Smoked Salmon and Potato Stacks

M a k e s   2 0

1kg / 2¼ lb potatoes, peeled and thinly sliced
500g / 1 lb 2 oz smoked salmon
salt and freshly ground black pepper
500ml / 16 fl oz vegetable stock (see page 79)

Preheat the oven to 190C / Gas 5.

Line a greased baking tray with two layers of potatoes, season lightly, then add a layer of smoked salmon, and then a small ladle of vegetable stock. Repeat these layers until all the potatoes, salmon and stock have been used, finishing with a layer of potato.

Cover with tin foil and bake for an hour until cooked through and tender. Weight with something heavy, then chill in refrigerator. To serve, cut into 1.5cm / ¾-inch squares.

❋ To make the cutting easier, line the baking tray with lightly-greased greaseproof paper before starting. At the end, you can then lift the whole dish out of the tray on to a cutting board.

19

Sushi

Makes approximately 25 pieces

Sushi Rice

3½ cups of short grain rice
4 cups water

≈

SUSHI VINEGAR
5 tablespoons rice vinegar
5 tablespoons sugar
4 teaspoons salt

Wash the rice in cold water three times to remove the excess starch. Bring to the boil and cook for 2 minutes, uncovered. Then let it simmer for 15-20 minutes in a lidded pan until the water has been absorbed.

While the rice is cooking, combine the vinegar, sugar and salt in a bowl. Ensure that all ingredients have dissolved.

Remove from the heat, take off the lid and let stand for 5 minutes, then fold the sugar and salt solution into the cooked rice. Cover with a clean kitchen towel and allow to stand for a further 5 minutes. The rice is now ready to use.

FILLINGS (10CM LENGTH X 1CM SQUARED)
raw salmon strips
raw tuna strips (remove dark meat)
cucumber strips (remove seeds)
carrot strips (boiled in hot water for 3 minutes, then refresh
*   in cold water until cold)*

Maki Sushi (Sushi Rolls)

Nori (dried Japanese seaweed sheets)
bowl of vinegared water
prepared rice
Wasabi (Japanese mustard)
fillings as above

The traditional way of creating maki sushi is to do it on a small bamboo mat. Place a sheet of Nori, shiny side down, on the mat. Wet your right hand in the vinegared water, take a ball of rice and spread it in an even layer over half of the Nori sheet. Spread a smear of Wasabi along the middle of the rice. Arrange the strips and pieces of vegetables and fish along the smear of Wasabi.

Lift the end of the mat and gently roll it over the ingredients, pressing gently to compact the rice. Roll it forward to make a complete roll.

Slice the rolls gently with a very sharp knife. Serve as soon as possible, so that the seaweed is still a bit crispy.

Temaki Sushi

Temaki is cone-shaped. Place a triangular half-sheet of Nori with one corner facing you, one facing away, and one to the left. Place a little rice and Wasabi by the left corner. Bring the far corner towards you, overlapping the near corner to make a cone, leaving a little of the filling showing.

Opposite: Maki Sushi

Filo Tartlets with Chargrilled Salmon, Ginger and Avocado

Makes 20

This colourful special-occasion starter looks so appetising when presented as an individual tartlet garnished with summer leaves. Bags of mixed salad leaves are, of course, readily available in supermarkets and are perfect for adding the finishing touch to the plate.

1 packet filo pastry
500g / 1 lb 2 oz salmon, sliced
25g / 1 oz fresh root ginger, finely grated
50ml / 3 tablespoons olive oil
1 avocado, diced
50g / 1¾ oz tomato, skinned, de-seeded and finely diced
50g / 1¾ oz yellow peppers, de-seeded and finely diced
½ bunch coriander, chopped
½ bunch basil, chopped
½ bunch dill for garnish

Preheat the oven to 220C / Gas 7.

Heat a griddle pan. Lightly brush the salmon with oil. Chargrill it for a minute or so each side, then flake and allow to cool. (If you haven't got a griddle pan, you can chargrill under a hot grill.)

Gently cook the ginger in a little of the olive oil until coloured, taking care not to burn it.

Mix the cooked salmon with the diced vegetables,

chopped herbs and ginger and 2 tablespoons olive oil. Brush the filo with the olive oil and cut into twenty 3cm / 1⅓-inch rounds. Push into small tartlet tins and bake for 6-8 minutes until golden.

To serve cold, fill the tartlets with the salmon mixture and add a garnish of dill.

To serve warm, gently heat the salmon mixture in a pan. Fill the tartlets and garnish with sprigs of dill.

Filo Tartlets with Black Olives, Cherry Tomatoes and Basil

Makes 20

1 packet filo pastry
500g / 1 lb 2 oz cherry tomatoes, skinned, de-seeded and diced
150g / 5½ oz pitted black olives, cut into quarters
2 bunches basil, finely chopped
75ml / 4 tablespoons virgin olive oil
freshly ground black pepper

Make the tartlets according to the previous recipe.

Mix together the tomatoes, olives, basil and olive oil, then leave to chill for 6 hours. Spoon into the tartlets, and serve immediately.

✤ It is essential to use good quality olives and ripe cherry tomatoes.

✤ Chef's Tip

Fold the salmon and avocado very carefully to keep its shape, and add the dressing at the last minute so that it does not seep into the pastry and make it soggy.

22

Vegetable Tempura

Serves 20

20 asparagus tips
20 broccoli florets
20 wild mushrooms, washed carefully
20 red pepper strips
20 thin sweet potato batons
200g / 7 oz tempura flour
800ml / 28 fl oz very cold fizzy water
vegetable oil for frying
pinch of chilli powder
salt and pepper

Mix together the flour and water to form a batter with the consistency of single cream. Mix in the chilli powder, salt and pepper.

Dip the vegetables in the batter, then deep-fry in oil heated to 220C for between 45 seconds and a minute, until very crisp.

Serve hot with a sweet chilli dipping sauce (see page 84) or soy sauce.

Root Vegetable Crisps

Using a vegetable peeler, simply peel slices of any root vegetable you like – such as parsnips, carrots, sweet potatoes, beetroot – and deep-fry in oil heated to 160C until the fryer has stopped bubbling and the vegetables are golden and crisp.

❄ Can be kept in an air-tight container for up to 1 week.

Bruschetta of Roasted Peppers, Anchovies and Capers

Serves 20

8 red peppers
40 fresh anchovy fillets
100ml / 4 fl oz olive oil
50g / 1¾ oz capers, drained and finely chopped
½ bunch basil, finely chopped
½ bunch coriander, finely chopped
ciabatta bread stick (cut into ½-inch rounds)

Preheat the oven to 250C / Gas 9, then roast the peppers for 10 minutes until the skins are blackened. Place in a plastic tub and tightly close (or use a bowl sealed with cling film). When cool enough to handle, skin, de-seed and cut into diamonds.

Using cocktail sticks, alternately skewer the anchovies and red pepper, two pieces of each per stick.

Warm the olive oil, add the capers and herbs, brush generously over the sliced ciabatta and toast under the grill.

Assemble skewered anchovies and peppers onto ciabatta bread and serve immediately.

Thai Chicken Satay

Makes 50

The distinctive flavours of lemon grass, lime leaves and chilli conjure up a taste of the Orient on neat, easy-to-handle skewers, which make satay an ideal canapé for entertaining. Thai cuisine is an increasingly popular choice for home entertaining, and Thai herbs and spices are now readily available in supermarkets.

6 chicken breasts, cut into thin strips
100g / 3½ oz chilli, chopped
50g / 2 oz garlic, chopped
50g / 2 oz lemon grass, chopped
1 bunch coriander
1 bunch basil
4 lime leaves
400g / 1 lb peanuts
200ml / 8 fl oz sesame oil
250ml / 10 fl oz coconut milk

Place all the ingredients, except for the chicken, in a food processor and blend to a fine paste.

Take half the satay marinade and warm it in a pan for 20 minutes. Allow to cool. This will be used as a dip.

Brush the rest of the marinade over the chicken pieces, then skewer them onto wooden skewers that have been previously soaked in water to prevent the wood burning. Cook under a medium-hot grill for 4 minutes each side or until the chicken is cooked through. Serve warm, with the satay dip.

❋ Chef's Tip

Leave the chicken pieces to soak up the flavours of the marinade for a while before cooking. For a more intense flavour they can be chargrilled – but it is messy!

Spring Rolls with a Sweet Chilli Dipping Sauce

Makes 50 - 60

1 packet spring roll pastry (available from Asian markets, or use filo pastry)
1 egg white
15ml / 1 tablespoon sesame oil
150g / 5½ oz leeks, cut into matchsticks
150g / 5½ oz carrots, cut into matchsticks
150g / 5½ oz bean sprouts
8g / ¼ oz chilli, chopped
8g / ¼ oz ginger, grated
½ bunch coriander, chopped
8g / ¼ oz sesame seeds
vegetable oil for frying
1 x Sweet Chilli Dipping Sauce recipe (see page 84)

Cut the pastry into 4cm / 1½-inch squares and brush with egg white. (If you are using filo pastry, brush with sesame oil.)

Mix together the rest of the ingredients, season with sesame oil, and place a teaspoonful of the mixture in the centre of each pastry square. Roll up, making sure you tuck in the ends.

Deep-fry in oil heated to 180C until golden. Drain well on kitchen paper and serve with sweet chilli dipping sauce.

❋ For a less fattening style, cook in a hot oven 220C / Gas 7 until brown.

Opposite, clockwise from bottom left:
Thai Chicken Satay, Spring Rolls with a
Sweet Chilli Dipping Sauce, Thai Fish Cakes

25

Goujons of Sole with Tartare Sauce

Serves 20

750g / 1 lb 11 oz lemon sole fillet
100g / 3½ oz seasoned flour
3 eggs, beaten
400g / 14 oz fresh white breadcrumbs
vegetable oil
1 x Tartare Sauce recipe (see page 83)

Cut the lemon sole into batons about the size of your little finger. Dip first in the seasoned flour, then in the egg, and then roll in the breadcrumbs. Chill in refrigerator for at least 15 minutes. (May be stored in freezer.)

Fry these goujons in very hot oil for 2 minutes until crisp and golden. Drain well on kitchen paper, season with salt, and serve with tartare sauce and a wedge of lemon.

Matchstick Chips

Serves 20

4 large bakers potatoes, peeled
oil for frying
salt

Slice the potatoes finely and then cut into matchsticks. Rinse in cold water and drain well. Deep-fry at 185C for 2 minutes until golden brown. Drain on kitchen paper. Season with salt.

Fish and Chips

Serves 20

1 x Goujons of Sole recipe
1 x Matchstick Chips recipe
1 x Tartare Sauce recipe (see page 83)

Prepare Goujons of Sole and Matchstick Chips as above and serve in paper cones with Tartare Sauce and lemon wedges to accompany.

Herb Sausages with Honey and Sesame Seeds

Makes 20

20 small herb sausages
175ml / 6 fl oz jar honey
20ml / 1 tablespoon soy sauce
50g / 1¾ oz black-and-white sesame seeds
100ml / 4 fl oz sesame oil

Grill or bake the sausages until golden. Mix the honey, soy sauce, sesame seeds and oil together, and place in a hot oven for 30 seconds.

Just before serving, pour the honey and sesame seed mixture over the sausages. Serve warm.

✳ A good-quality herb mustard goes well as a dip.

Opposite: Fish and Chips

26

27

28

Duck in Pancakes

Makes 20 pancakes

2 large (1.35kg / 3 lb) ducks
100ml / 4 fl oz honey
20g / ¾ oz fresh root ginger
8g / ¼ oz coriander seeds
200ml / 7 fl oz pineapple juice
30ml / 1½ tablespoons rice wine vinegar
50ml / 3 tablespoons soy sauce
1 bunch spring onions, cut into julienne strips
1 large cucumber, peeled and cut into julienne strips
20 Chinese pancakes

Preheat the oven to 100C / Gas ¼, then roast the ducks for 6 hours in a deep roasting tray on a wire rack. When handling, be careful of the hot fat which will run into the pan.

Place the honey, ginger, coriander seeds, pineapple juice, wine vinegar and soy sauce in a pan, bring to the boil and simmer for 5 minutes.

Take the ducks out of the oven and drain the fat from the pan. This can be kept in the refrigerator and used in other recipes such as Confit of Duck (page 104).

Pour half of the honey and ginger sauce over the ducks.

Increase oven temperature to 230C / Gas 8. Roast for a further 20-25 minutes until the ducks are golden and crispy.

Allow the ducks to cool, then shred the meat, mix with the spring onions and cucumber and the rest of the sauce and wrap in warmed Chinese pancakes. Serve with Hoisin sauce, which is available from supermarkets and delis.

✣ The traditional Chinese way to serve this dish is to put all the ingredients separately on the table and let guests help themselves.

Opposite: Duck in Pancakes

Thai Fish Cakes

Makes 40 fish cakes

The modern gefilte fish ball! A very popular dish and a good alternative if you want to break from tradition and offer your guests something a little different. These spicy fish cakes also work well as part of an Oriental themed canapé selection with other dishes such as sushi, spring rolls and Thai chicken satay. Scrumptious and very trendy.

1kg / 2¼ lb white fish fillet (such as coley, cod or haddock)
100g / 3½ oz breadcrumbs
50g / 1¾ oz ground almonds
12g / ½ oz chopped basil, mint and coriander
2.5g / ¹⁄₁₆ oz chopped chilli
2.5g / ¹⁄₁₆ oz chopped garlic
4g / ⅛ oz chopped ginger
2.5g / ¹⁄₁₆ oz chopped lemon grass
2.5g / ¹⁄₁₆ oz chopped lime leaves
25ml / 1½ tablespoons lemon juice
50ml / 2 fl oz light soy sauce
salt and pepper

Mince the fish in a food processor, then mix with the rest of the ingredients, cover and leave overnight in the fridge.

Mould into small rounds and fry in oil or margarine until golden brown on each side and cooked through.

Serve with a sweet chilli dipping sauce (see page 84).

✣ A little coconut cream can be used to sweeten the mixture.

✣ Chef's Tip
Best served warm rather than hot to appreciate the intense mix of flavours.

29

Breaded Chicken Goujons

M A K E S   3 0 - 4 0

4 chicken breasts

Follow the method given for Goujons of Sole (see page 26), replacing the fish with strips of chicken breast. Serve with deep-fried Matchstick Chips (see page 26) in paper cones.

✳ You can always vary the recipe by adding different combinations of herbs, poppy seeds, sesame seeds, chopped parsley, etc. to the breadcrumb mix.

Carpaccio of Beef with Lemon and Olive Oil

S E R V E S   2 0
(or 4 as a starter)

500g / 1 lb 2 oz beef fillet (trimmed rib eye)
100ml / 4 fl oz olive oil
zest and juice of 2 lemons
salt and freshly ground black pepper
bread for toasting

Ask your butcher to trim the beef and slice it paper thin. Marinate it in the olive oil and lemon zest and juice for 2 hours.

Just prior to serving, season the beef with coarse sea salt, black pepper and lemon juice.

Serve on toasted bread.

Mini Burgers in a Bun

M A K E S   2 0

500g / 1 lb 2 oz minced beef
25g / 1 oz shallots, chopped
5g / ⅛ oz chopped thyme and rosemary
5g / ⅛ oz minced garlic
1 egg, beaten
50g / 1¾ oz breadcrumbs
salt and freshly ground black pepper
a squeeze of lemon juice
20 mini burger buns

Mix together the minced beef, shallots, herbs, garlic, egg and breadcrumbs, season with salt and pepper to taste, and add a squeeze of lemon juice.

Shape into approximately 20 mini burgers.

Either grill or fry until cooked through, for about 5 or 6 minutes.

Serve the burgers in mini burger buns accompanied by matchstick chips (see page 26), a slice of gherkin and a drizzle of tomato ketchup or mustard.

30

Mini Hot Dogs with Fried Onions

Makes 20

20 mini hot dogs
2 large onions, thinly sliced
oil or margarine for frying
20 mini finger rolls

Heat the hot dogs according to the packet instructions.

Just before serving, fry the onions in a little oil or margarine until golden.

Place the hot dogs in the buns and top with the onions. Serve with spicy tomato sauce (see page 81).

Crudités with a Garlic and Dill Mayonnaise

Serves 6

20 baby carrots
20 asparagus tips
20 broccoli florets
20 radishes
20 red pepper batons
20 baby sweetcorn
20 cherry tomatoes
20 batons peeled celery
1 x Garlic and Dill Mayonnaise recipe (see page 84)

Trim all the vegetables to a uniform size. Lightly blanch the asparagus tips and the broccoli, and cool them in iced water. Serve with a garlic and dill mayonnaise.

Mini Potato Latkes

Makes 32 latkes

2 lb potatoes (peeled)
4 oz onions
2 eggs
4 oz flour
salt and freshly ground black pepper

Cut the potatoes and onions into small dice. Mince and drain through a colander. Add eggs, salt and pepper, then flour. Drain in a colander.

Preheat the deep fryer to 160C . Once the oil has reached the temperature, with a teaspoon place an oval shape of the mixture into the hot oil and allow to cook until light brown, making sure the inside is thoroughly cooked. Remove from oil and drain.

To serve, put the oil up to 180C and place the half-cooked latkes into the oil for approximately 1 minute. Remove from oil, sprinkle with salt to taste, and serve.

31

Carole Sobell's

Soups and Starters

33

Opposite: Teriyaki Salmon Wrapped in Filo

Traditional Chicken Soup

Serves 4 - 6

Everyone's mum makes the best chicken soup, and when you're feeling a little under the weather there's nothing to beat a warm and comforting bowl of this great classic. Passed down from generation to generation, it has never been beaten and never bettered – it is, after all, the Jewish penicillin!

a whole or half chicken or fowl with the wings and giblets
2 teaspoons salt
a pinch of white pepper
1 large onion, peeled and halved
2 large carrots, peeled and halved
2 sticks celery, leaves and top 2 inches (5cm) only
1 sprig of parsley
any soft eggs from inside the fowl (if used)
80g / 3 oz lockshen (vermicelli)

≈

FOR THE DUMPLINGS
1 pack Telma Kneidlach mix
(available from supermarkets and delis)

Put the bird, wings and giblets in a large, heavy soup pan with 1.75 litres / 3 pints water, add the salt and pepper, cover and bring to the boil, skimming off any froth with a large, wet metal spoon.

Add the onion, carrots, celery, parsley and eggs, if using. Bring back to the boil, then reduce the heat so that the liquid is barely bubbling. Cover and continue to simmer for a further 3 hours or so, either on top of the stove or in a slow oven at Gas 2 / 150C, until the chicken feels very tender when a leg is prodded with a fork.

Strain the soup into a large bowl, reserving the carrots in a separate container. Cover the soup and place it in the refrigerator overnight.

Next day, remove any congealed fat and return the soup to the pan. (If there is a thick layer of fat, it can be heated in a pan to drive off any liquid and then, when it has stopped bubbling, cooled and stored like rendered raw fat.)

Make the dumplings according to packet instructions.

Cut the carrots into small dice, and add them to the pan. Finally, add approximately ½ oz / 15g per person of lockshen cooked in boiling water according to the packet directions.

Add the dumplings and reheat the soup slowly before serving.

❄ The soup will keep for three days in the refrigerator or for up to three months in the freezer.

❄ Chef's Tip

Note that this traditional recipe requires you to make the soup the day before you use it. But if you want to cut corners, you can leave that bit out!

Opposite: Traditional Chicken Soup

Carole Sobell's

Roast Tomato Soup with Fresh Basil

S e r v e s   4 - 6

A beautiful, light and versatile soup which is equally suitable served before fish, chicken or meat dishes. Choose a good, flavoursome tomato such as plum or one of the vine-ripened varieties. Roasting the tomatoes concentrates the flavours even further, and with the addition of fresh basil the soup takes on the wonderful tastes of summer.

2kg / 4½ lb ripe vine tomatoes
6 cloves garlic
12 large shallots, peeled
150ml / 5 fl oz olive oil
250ml / 8 fl oz vegetable stock (see page 79)
50g / 2 tablespoons tomato paste (purée)
2 large bunches basil, leaves and stalks separated
salt and freshly ground black pepper

Preheat the oven to 250C / Gas 9.

Place the tomatoes on a large roasting tray with the garlic and shallots, pour over the olive oil, season with a good pinch of salt, and roast for 25 minutes until the edges of the tomatoes begin to blacken.

Remove the tomato stalks and discard.

Put the tomatoes, garlic, shallots and the juice into a large pan with the vegetable stock, add the basil stalks and tomato paste, and simmer for 20 minutes. Allow to

✳ Style Tip

Serve the soup in deep round bowls which have been warmed in the oven, place on a plate garnished with garden leaves and add thick crusty bread.

✳ Chef's Tip

Add chopped fresh basil at the last minute to retain the full flavour of the herb.

cool slightly, then liquidise and pass through a fine sieve. Return to pan, adjust consistency, and season to taste. Cornflour mixed with a little cold water can be added to thicken the liquid.

Just before serving, garnish with shredded basil leaves and drizzle with a little olive oil.

Wild Mushroom Soup

S e r v e s   8 - 1 0

2 garlic cloves, finely chopped
6 shallots, finely chopped
50g / 1¾ oz margarine
400g / 14 oz wild mushrooms, wiped clean and
     roughly chopped
800ml / 28 fl oz brown chicken stock (see page 80)
1 tablespoon cornflour
1 bunch chives, finely chopped

In a saucepan with a lid, gently sweat the garlic and shallots in the margarine over a low heat until soft but not coloured.

Add the mushrooms and cook slowly for 8 minutes.

Add the stock and simmer for 5 minutes.

Mix the cornflour with a little cold water, add to the soup and cook for a further 5 minutes.

Liquidise and pass through a sieve. Return to the heat and adjust seasoning and consistency.

Just before serving, sprinkle with the chives.

Cream of Vegetable Soup with Garlic Croûtons

Serves 10 - 12

50g / 1¾ oz leek, sliced
100g / 3½ oz onion, cut into 1cm / ½-inch dice
2 garlic cloves, chopped
50g / 1¾ oz margarine
50ml / 3 tablespoons olive oil
100g / 3½ oz carrots, cut into 1cm / ½-inch dice
50g / 1¾ oz celery, cut into 1cm / ½-inch dice
50g / 1¾ oz celeriac, cut into 1cm / ½-inch dice
150g / 5½ oz potatoes, cut into 1cm / ½-inch dice
800ml / 28 fl oz vegetable stock (see page 79)
8g / ¼ oz salt
1 bunch parsley, finely chopped

≈

FOR THE GARLIC CROÛTONS
8 cloves garlic
1 baguette
200ml / 7 fl oz olive oil

Preheat the oven to 160C / Gas 3.

Sweat the leek, onion and garlic in the margarine and olive oil in a large pan with a lid for 5 minutes on a moderate heat.

Add the remaining vegetables, stock and salt and simmer, with the lid on, for 45 minutes. Allow to cool slightly, liquidise and pass through a sieve. Add salt and pepper to taste.

To make garlic croûtons: Cut the baguette into 1cm / ½-inch squares and in a bowl mix together with the whole garlic cloves, olive oil and a big pinch of rock salt. Place the croûtons and garlic on a baking sheet and bake

in the oven for 30 minutes or until crunchy and golden.

Adjust the seasoning of the soup to taste, reheat, then serve with the garlic croûtons and parsley.

Pumpkin Soup with Truffle Oil

Serves 4

1 leek, sliced
1 onion, chopped
oil or margarine for frying
1 large pumpkin, skinned, de-seeded and diced
500ml / 16 fl oz vegetable stock (see page 79)
salt and freshly ground black pepper
truffle oil (available from supermarkets and delicatessens)

37

In a lidded saucepan, cook the leek and onion in a little oil or margarine until soft, but not coloured. Add the pumpkin and cook for about 5 minutes until tender.

Add half the stock, season with salt and pepper, bring to the boil, and simmer for 10 minutes.

Allow the soup to cool slightly, then liquidise and pass through a sieve.

Adjust the seasoning and texture to taste, adding more stock if you prefer a thinner soup.

Serve very hot with a drizzle of truffle oil.

Pea and Mint Soup

Serves 6

1 onion, chopped
oil or margarine for frying
500g / 1 lb 2 oz potatoes, peeled and diced
800ml / 28 fl oz vegetable stock (see page 79)
400g / 14 oz shelled fresh peas
1 bunch of mint, leaves and stalks separated
salt and freshly ground black pepper

Heat a little oil or margarine in a large pan with a lid and sweat the onion until soft. Add the diced potato and cook slowly for 5 minutes, stirring to prevent sticking.

Pour in the stock, add the peas and the mint stalks, season with salt and pepper, then bring to the boil and simmer for 10 minutes.

Allow the soup to cool slightly, then liquidise and pass through a fine sieve.

Adjust the seasoning and texture to taste, adding more vegetable stock if you prefer a thinner soup.

Finely chop the mint leaves, stir into the soup and serve immediately.

Borscht

Serves 6

2 onions
2 sticks celery, thinly sliced
¼ white cabbage
5 pints chicken stock
6 small beetroot, raw, finely diced
juice of 1 lemon
3 boiled potatoes, finely diced
200ml / ½ pint soya milk
sugar to taste
salt and freshly ground black pepper

Sweat the onions, celery and cabbage in the oil for five minutes, taking care not to let them brown.

Add the stock, bring to the boil, and simmer for 45 minutes. Strain through a fine sieve and return the liquid to the boil.

Add the finely-diced beetroot and lemon juice. Cook for a further 45 minutes.

Remove from the heat. When slightly cooled, add the finely diced potatoes, milk and sugar.

Heat slowly to serving temperature, add salt and pepper to taste, and serve.

✳ The borscht can be liquidised for a smooth texture, as in the photograph opposite. My mother always serves the potatoes chunky.

Opposite: Pumpkin Soup (left),
Pea and Mint Soup (centre), Borscht (right)

39

Bean and Barley Soup

Serves 10 - 12

100g / 3½ oz dried white haricot beans,
or 200g / 7 oz canned, drained
100g / 3½ oz carrots
100g / 3½ oz parsnips
100g / 3½ oz swede
100g / 3½ oz onion
100ml / 4 fl oz olive oil
85g / 3 oz pearl barley
2 cloves garlic, chopped
800ml / 28 fl oz brown chicken stock (see page 80)
10 sage leaves, chopped
1 sprig tarragon, chopped
2 sprigs parsley, chopped

If using dried beans, soak them overnight.

Peel and dice all the carrot, parsnip, swede and onion the same size as the haricot beans.

Heat the olive oil in a heavy-based, lidded saucepan, add the vegetables and garlic and colour gently for 5 minutes, stirring occasionally.

Add the stock and haricot beans, and simmer gently, with the lid on, for 45 minutes, skimming occasionally. Add the pearl barley and cook for a further 45 minutes until barley and beans are cooked. If, after this time, the beans are still hard, cook for a further 15 minutes or so.

Just before serving, add the herbs.

Roast Parsnip and Apple Soup

Serves 4

100ml / 4 fl oz vegetable oil
250g / 8½ oz parsnips, diced
250g / 8½ oz apples, peeled and diced
100g / 3½ oz onion, diced
2 cloves garlic, chopped
800ml / 40 fl oz chicken stock (see page 80)
quarter of a bunch of rosemary
salt and freshly ground pepper

In a large heavy-based pan, heat the vegetable oil until very hot. Add the parsnips, apples, onions, rosemary and garlic, and brown carefully, without burning, for 5-10 minutes.

When the vegetables are nicely browned and starting to break down, add the stock. Season, bring to the boil, and simmer for 30 minutes until the vegetables are very soft.

Allow to cool slightly, then liquidise, pass through a sieve and return to a clean pan. Adjust the seasoning and consistency according to taste, reheat and serve.

❊ Chef's Tip

Season soups with salt and pepper just before serving. With creamy or fish soups use a little lemon juice to help bring out the flavours.

Minestrone

Serves 6

75ml / 4 tablespoons olive oil

75g / 2½ oz onion, diced

2 garlic cloves, finely chopped

750ml / 27 fl oz brown chicken stock (see page 80)

50g / 1¾ oz carrot, diced

25g / 1 oz fresh peas, shelled

50g / 1¾ oz potatoes, diced the size of the peas

50g / 1¾ oz dried spaghetti, broken into
*   2cm / 1¾-inch pieces*

25g / 1 oz fresh broad beans, peeled and shelled

200g / 7 oz tomatoes, skinned, de-seeded and
*   diced the size of the peas*

1 bunch chives, finely chopped

Heat the olive oil in a large lidded pan and cook the carrot, onion and garlic until soft but not coloured.

Add the stock and simmer for 5 minutes.

Add the peas, potatoes and spaghetti and simmer for a further 10 minutes.

Add the broad beans and tomatoes and simmer for another 5 minutes.

Just before serving, add the chives.

❉ May be served with garlic croûtons – see page 37.

Trio of Soups

Serves 6

12 large shallots, finely sliced

6 cloves garlic, finely sliced

75ml / 3fl oz olive oil

9 green peppers, de-seeded and finely sliced

9 red peppers, de-seeded and finely sliced

9 yellow peppers, de-seeded and finely sliced

800ml / 28fl oz vegetable stock (see page 79)

Divide the shallots and garlic between three lidded pans and cook gently in the olive oil until soft but not coloured.

Add the green pepper to the first of the pans, the red to the second and the yellow to the last, and cook gently for 5 minutes.

Add a third of the vegetable stock to each of the pans, season, and simmer for a further 5 minutes.

Allow to cool slightly, liquidise each of the soups separately, washing the liquidiser in between, then return to three separate clean pans.

Adjust the seasoning to taste, and add a little more stock if necessary, so they each have a similar texture.

Reheat to boiling point. Pour into warm soup plates – three soups in each plate – so they have a swirled effect.

41

❉ Style Tip

To swirl the trio of soups together properly,
you really need two people! The first person
holds two pans of soup, the second holds one pan
of soup and a cocktail stick. Pour all three soups
into each soup plate at once, while stirring
them together on the plate with the cocktail stick.

Ribbons of Smoked Salmon with Roasted Vegetables

Serves 4

200g / 7 oz ribbons of smoked salmon
4 baby fennel
100ml / 4 fl oz olive oil
4 baby chicory, cut in half lengthways
4 baby aubergines, cut in half lengthways
4 baby courgettes, cut in half lengthways
100g / 3½ oz cherry tomatoes
salt and freshly ground black pepper
50ml / 3 tablespoons (12-year-old) balsamic vinegar

Preheat the oven to 250C / Gas 9.

Cook the fennel for 10 minutes in boiling salted water. Drain and dry thoroughly.

Heat a large roasting tray, then put in the olive oil. Add the vegetables, a good pinch of salt and some pepper, and roast for 10 minutes.

Add the vinegar and roast for a further 10 minutes.

Remove the vegetables from the oven and place in a plastic lidded tub, along with all the juices. Leave to infuse overnight.

Divide the vegetables between four small bowls, top with the smoked salmon ribbons and serve.

❋ For a final flourish, drizzle with balsamic vinaigrette.

Crown of Melon with a Cascade of Berry Fruits

Serves 4

2 ripe melons (such as Galia, honeydew or canteloupe)
100g / 3½ oz raspberries
100g / 3½ oz strawberries
100g / 3½ oz redcurrants
100g / 3½ oz blueberries
8g / ¼ oz fresh mint leaves

Cut each melon in half in a 'zig zag' style, and scoop out the seeds.

Wash and trim the soft fruit, then hull and halve the strawberries.

Spoon the soft fruit on top of each melon half. Shred the mint leaves and sprinkle over.

Opposite: Crown of Melon with a
Cascade of Berry Fruits

42

Teriyaki Salmon

Serves 4

4 x 100g / 3½ oz salmon portions
200ml / 7 fl oz teriyaki sauce (available from
*   supermarkets and delicatessans)*
4 wooden kebab skewers
1 leek, thinly sliced
1 courgette, cut into matchsticks
100g / 3½ oz bean sprouts
1 red pepper, de-seeded and thinly sliced
1 x Sesame and Chilli Dressing recipe (see page 84)

Cut each of the four salmon portions into about nine equal slices, and push onto wooden kebab skewers that have previously been soaked in water. Place in the teriyaki marinade and leave overnight.

Grill the salmon kebabs under a preheated grill for 3 minutes, until the skin is just crisp.

Stir-fry the vegetables with a little of the teriyaki marinade, and the sesame and chilli dressing, for 1 minute.

Spoon the stir-fried vegetables onto individual plates, and place a salmon kebab on top. Serve with the remaining sesame and chilli dressing on the side.

Opposite: Teriyaki Salmon

Teriyaki Salmon Wrapped in Filo

Serves 4

4 x 100g / 3½ oz salmon portions, thinly sliced
200ml / 7 fl oz teriyaki sauce (available from supermarkets
*   and delicatessens)*
1 leek, cut into matchsticks
1 courgette, cut into matchsticks
1 large carrot, cut into matchsticks
8 sheets filo pastry
50g / 1¾ oz bean sprouts
50ml / 3 tablespoons sesame oil
50ml / 3 tablespoons chilli sauce
50ml / 3 tablespoons coriander pesto (see page 82)

Marinate the salmon overnight in the refrigerator in 100ml of the teriyaki sauce.

Preheat the oven to 230C / Gas 8.

Heat a wok or large frying pan and stir-fry the leek, courgette, carrot and bean sprouts with 50ml of the teriyaki sauce. Allow to cool.

Brush two large pieces of filo with sesame oil. Place a tablespoon of the stir-fried vegetables on the pastry, cover with the slices of salmon, and fold the filo round and over to make a parcel.

Bake for 8 minutes, or until golden brown.

Meanwhile, warm the remaining vegetables, then spoon them onto the middle of a warm plate. Place the filo parcel on top, and drizzle the chilli sauce, pesto and remaining teriyaki sauce around it to garnish.

✳ *Photograph on page 32*

45

46

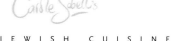

Chargrilled Salmon and Baby Leek Terrine with Saffron and Chive Dressing

Serves 8 - 10

8 bunches of baby leeks
1.6 litres / 2¾ pints vegetable stock (see page 79)
2 very large leeks, cut in half lengthways
800g / 1¾ lb salmon fillets
2 x sachets aga aga (gelatine substitute, available in
*   supermarkets and delicatessens)*
pinch of saffron
1 x Saffron and Chive Dressing recipe (see page 84)
100ml / 4 fl oz olive oil
100g / 4 oz mixed peppers, diced, to garnish

Take a 24 x 10cm / 9½ x 4-inch terrine mould and line it with cling film.

Simmer the baby leeks for 8 minutes in 1 litre / 1¾ pints of the stock. Using a slotted spoon, lift from the stock, then allow to cool. Add the large leeks to the stock and blanch for 1 minute. Drain, allow to cool, dry with a cloth, then split into ribbons.

Slice the salmon fillet into 3 equal long thin slices, about 8mm / ¼ inch thick (or ask your fishmonger to do this).

Preheat a griddle pan until very hot, brush the salmon with the olive oil, then chargrill on one side only, for 2 minutes or so, taking care not to over-cook the fish. Leave to cool.

Warm the remaining vegetable stock and add the aga aga and saffron. Allow to cool slightly.

Lay some of the large leeks in the bottom of the terrine, put a layer of salmon on top, drizzle over some of the warm vegetable stock, then add a layer of the baby leeks. Repeat these layers until you reach the top of the mould, finishing with a layer of the large leeks.

Cover with cling film, put a weight such as a small chopping board on top of the terrine, and leave in the refrigerator overnight.

Lift the terrine from the mould, using the cling film to help you. With a hot knife, cut a slice and serve with chopped peppers and the chive dressing drizzled around it.

Chargrilled Asparagus

Serves 6

3 large bunches of asparagus
100ml / 4 fl oz olive oil

Preheat the grill until very hot.

Trim the ends of the asparagus, and peel if hard or woody. Dip the asparagus in the olive oil, making sure they are well coated, then place under the grill until lightly charred. Serve either warm or cold.

Opposite: Chargrilled Asparagus

Tower of Roasted Vegetables

Serves 4

Presentation is the key to this colourful combination of roasted vegetables which should be succulent but still have some bite. Serve on attractive large plates and stack high to feed the eyes first.

1 aubergine, sliced into 1cm rounds

2 courgettes, sliced into 1cm rounds

1 sprig thyme

1 sprig rosemary

2 cloves garlic, crushed

100ml / 4 fl oz olive oil

4 red peppers

2 onions, peeled and sliced into 1cm / ½-inch rings

1 x Pesto Sauce recipe (see page 82)

1 x Spicy Tomato Sauce recipe (see page 81)

Marinate the aubergine and courgette in a mixture of the thyme, rosemary, garlic and olive oil and leave for a minimum of 2 hours.

Meanwhile, roast the peppers in an oven preheated to 250C / Gas 9 for 10 minutes. When cool enough to handle, remove the blackened skins, de-seed, and cut into discs.

Heat a stove-top griddle pan or preheat a grill. Remove the courgette and aubergine slices from the marinade (setting this aside until later) and chargrill them together with the onion and the roasted peppers.

Place the chargrilled vegetables in an ovenproof dish, cover with the reserved marinade, and bake uncovered in an oven preheated to 160C / Gas 3 for 20 minutes.

On each of the four serving plates, layer the vegetables on top of each other to form a tower. Garnish each plate with drizzles of pesto and spicy tomato sauce. Serve warm.

Opposite: Tower of Roasted Vegetables

✳ Style Tip

Dust the serving plates with a sprinkling of paprika through a sieve to add a perfect finishing touch.

Mosaic of Provençal Vegetables with Pesto

Serves 12

Imagine a long, lazy summer Sunday lunch, relaxing with great friends and good wine and you have it all summed up in this superbly colourful dish. If you use fresh pesto sauce, it does take a little time and effort to prepare, but then what else will you have to do but sit back with family and friends and enjoy!

2 sachets aga aga (gelatine substitute, available in supermarkets and delicatessens)
1 x Spicy Tomato Sauce recipe (see page 81)
10 red peppers
20 large spinach leaves, washed and stalks removed
4 large aubergines
4 fennel bulbs
6 large courgettes, cut in quarters lengthways
15 large ripe plum tomatoes, skinned and de-seeded
1 x Pesto Sauce recipe (see page 82)

Preheat the oven to 250C / Gas 9.

Add the aga aga to the warm spicy tomato sauce, following the manufacturer's instructions.

Roast the red peppers for 10 minutes until the skins are blackened. When cool enough to handle, skin, de-seed and slice. Reduce the oven temperature to 180C / Gas 4.

Blanch the spinach for 10 seconds in boiling salted water, refresh in cold water, then dry using a tea towel.

Wrap the aubergines in aluminium foil and bake for 30 minutes. Allow to cool, then slice.

Cook the fennel bulbs in boiling salted water for 15 minutes, refresh in cold water, then finely slice.

Pan-fry the courgettes in a little oil or margarine until golden.

✳ Chef's Tip

Fresh pesto sauce begins to lose some of its strength after about two hours – for maximum flavour impact, serve around 20 minutes after preparing.

Line a 24 x 10cm / 9½ x 4-inch terrine mould or rectangular bread tin with cling film, and then with some of the blanched spinach leaves, ensuring that the leaves overlap.

Put a ladle of warm tomato sauce in the bottom of the terrine, then a layer of aubergine. Add another ladle of warm tomato sauce, followed by a layer of red pepper.

Continue with a ladle of warm tomato sauce, followed by the courgette. A ladle of warm tomato sauce then the tomato. A ladle of warm tomato sauce, followed by fennel, finishing with the spinach.

Cover with cling film, put a weight such as a small chopping board on top of the terrine, and refrigerate for at least 24 hours.

To serve, lift the terrine out of the mould using the cling film to help you. Heat the blade of a knife in hot water, cut a slice and place in the middle of a 'pool' of pesto sauce on a large cold plate.

50

Warm Spinach and Mushroom Tartlets with Spicy Tomato Sauce

Serves 4

500g / 1 lb 2 oz spinach, washed and stalks removed
150g / 5½ oz mushrooms, washed and sliced
25g / 1 oz margarine
100ml / 4 fl oz soya milk
3 eggs
1 bunch chives, chopped
salt
1 x Spicy Tomato Sauce recipe (see page 81)

≈

FOR THE PASTRY
250g / 8½ oz flour
5g / 1 level teaspoon salt
160g / 5¾ oz margarine, cut into pieces
1 egg
10ml / 2 teaspoons water

Make the pastry by putting the flour, margarine and salt in a food processor, then pulse until it resembles breadcrumbs. Add the egg and water and pulse again until a dough has formed. Wrap in cling film and allow to rest for 2 hours.

Preheat the oven to 220C / Gas 7.

Roll out the pastry on a lightly-floured surface and use to line four 10cm / 4-inch tartlet cases. Bake blind for 20 minutes (see page 151). Reduce oven to 190C / Gas 5.

Blanch the spinach in boiling salted water for 2 minutes, drain, allow to cool, then dry with a cloth. Sauté the mushrooms in the margarine. Leave to cool.

Whisk the milk, eggs and most of the chives together with a large pinch of salt. Divide the spinach and mushroom between the four tartlets and pour over the egg mixture.

Bake until just set – about 10 minutes. Serve on a bed of leaves with spicy tomato sauce; sprinkle with chopped chives.

Tartare of Smoked Salmon

Serves 4 - 6

400g / 14 oz smoked salmon, in a piece
1 cucumber
8 small plum tomatoes, skinned and de-seeded
1 avocado
100ml / 4 fl oz mayonnaise (see page 82)
1 bunch dill, finely chopped
1 bunch chives, finely chopped

51

Cut the smoked salmon into slices 2mm / ⅛-inch thick and then dice into 2mm / ⅛-inch cubes. Peel the cucumber, cut in half lengthways, de-seed. Slice one half very thinly. Dice the other half into 2mm / ⅛-inch cubes. Dice the tomato and avocado in the same way.

Mix together mayonnaise and herbs. Use half of this to bind together the diced ingredients. Divide the mixture into 4-6 pastry cutters (these are available at any cookshop).

Spread the remaining mayonnaise with herbs on top of the salmon mixture, and garnish with the sliced cucumber. Chill for 4 hours until set. Place one cutter on each plate, loosen the sides with a knife, and carefully lift off.

Serve with toasted bread.

Carole Sobell's

Pasta and Risottos

Opposite: Linguine of Slow Roast Vegetables

Tagliatelle with Wild Mushrooms and Artichokes

Serves 4

4 tablespoons olive oil
4 tablespoons diced shallot
1 clove garlic, diced
400g / 1 lb wild mushrooms, diced
4 large artichokes, trimmed and outer leaves discarded
800g / 1¾ lb fresh tagliatelle
4 tablespoons chopped chives
a pinch of picked thyme
pesto oil and fresh basil to garnish

Heat the olive oil in a pan and fry the shallot, thyme and garlic until golden. Add the wild mushrooms and continue to fry until these too are golden.

Cook the artichokes in boiling salted water for 10 minutes until tender. Drain, then refresh in iced water. Peel off the leaves, remove the choke and slice. Add to the mushroom mixture.

Cook the tagliatelle according to the packet instructions.

Toss all the ingredients together, then divide between four bowls. Garnish with shredded basil leaves and a drizzle of pesto oil.

Linguine of Slow Roast Vegetables

Serves 4 - 6

200g / 7 oz vine tomatoes
12 cloves garlic
100g / 3½ oz fine green beans
4 red peppers
4 yellow mild chillies
4 baby aubergines
4 baby fennel bulbs
4 small courgettes, cut into batons
100ml / 4 fl oz olive oil
50ml / 3 tablespoons balsamic vinegar
200g / 7 oz packet fresh linguine

Preheat the oven to 190C / Gas 5.

Leave the tomatoes whole, including the stalks. Peel the garlic cloves. Cut all the other vegetables to a uniform size so they will cook evenly. Mix well with the oil and vinegar in a roasting tray, and roast for 45 minutes.

Cook the pasta according to the instructions on the packet, drain well, twist round a fork and place in the middle of a large warm platter. Spoon the roast vegetables around the outside and drizzle over the cooking juices.

✳ *Photograph on page 52*

✳ Chef's Tip

To enhance both the flavour and the aesthetics of the linguine, you can drizzle round pesto oil and Spicy Tomato Sauce (see page 81)

Opposite: Slow Roast Vegetables

54

NEW JEWISH CUISINE

Open Ravioli of Salmon with Chive Velouté

Serves 4

This delicate-tasting dish can be served as either a starter or a main course. The use of soya milk does not impair the flavour and means it can be served with a meat meal. It's also a useful healthy alternative for anyone opting for a dairy-free diet.

400g / 14 oz salmon, thinly sliced
1 bunch of chives, finely chopped

≈

FOR THE PASTA DOUGH
450g / 1 lb strong flour
5 eggs
15g / ½ oz salt
2 tablespoons olive oil

≈

FOR THE VELOUTÉ
50g / 1¾ oz margarine
50g / 1¾ oz flour
500ml / 16 fl oz soya milk
Salt and pepper to taste

To make the pasta, place all the ingredients for the dough in a food processor and blend until the mixture resembles fine breadcrumbs. Turn out on to a lightly-floured surface and knead until smooth. Wrap in cling film and allow to rest for 2 hours.

Using a pasta machine, roll out the dough until you reach the finest setting (or roll on a lightly-floured surface until paper-thin). Cut into 20 squares of 5cm / 2 inches each.

To make the velouté, melt the margarine in a pan, then add the flour and stir until thickened. Add the milk, a little at a time, stirring continuously until all the milk has been absorbed and you have a smooth sauce. Continue stirring whilst simmering for 5 minutes, then strain into a clean pan. Season to taste, if you prefer

Blanch the pasta squares in boiling salted water for 2 minutes, then drain well.

Preheat the grill.

Arrange the slices of salmon on top of the pasta squares in a large, warm, shallow dish. Flash the salmon and pasta squares under the grill for 1 minute or until the salmon turns opaque.

Bring the sauce back to the boil, add most of the chives, spoon over the ravioli and serve with a sprinkling of chopped chives.

✳ Style Tip

Best served in shallow soup plates for eye appeal and easy eating.

57

Opposite: Open Ravioli of Salmon with Chive Velouté

Pumpkin Risotto

Serves 4

1 tablespoon olive oil
50g / 1¾ oz margarine
1 clove garlic, finely chopped
2 shallots, diced
300g / 10½ oz pumpkin, skinned, de-seeded and diced
350g / 12 oz risotto rice
250ml / 8 fl oz dry white wine
1.25 litres / 45 fl oz chicken stock (see page 80)
chives to garnish

Heat the olive oil and margarine in a large pan and sweat the shallots and garlic until soft, then add the pumpkin and cook for 5 minutes or until tender.

Add the rice and the wine to the pumpkin mixture and cook for a further 5 minutes.

Add the chicken stock a ladle at a time, stirring continuously and waiting until all the liquid has been absorbed before adding more. Do this for 15-20 minutes, until the rice is just cooked.

Garnish with chopped chives and serve immediately.

✳ For a fun effect, you can serve this in a hollowed-out baby squash.

Vegetable Risotto

Serves 4

2 tablespoons olive oil
50g / 1¾ oz margarine
2 shallots, finely diced
2 cloves garlic, chopped
350g / 12 oz risotto rice
250ml / 8 fl oz dry white wine
1 red pepper, peeled and diced
1 aubergine, diced
1.25 litres / 43 fl oz vegetable stock (see page 79)
1 courgette, chopped
100g / 3½ oz plum tomatoes, diced
chives to garnish

Heat the olive oil and margarine in a large pan and sweat the shallots and garlic until soft. Add the rice and the wine and cook for a further 5 minutes.

Add the pepper and aubergine and cook for 5 minutes or until tender.

Add the stock, a ladle at a time, stirring continuously, and waiting until all the liquid is absorbed before adding more. Do this for approximately 10 minutes.

Add the rest of the vegetables and continue to ladle the stock for 5-10 minutes, until the rice is just cooked.

Serve sprinkled with chopped chives.

58

Wild Mushroom Risotto (recipe page 61)

Wild Mushroom Risotto

Serves 4

Most supermarkets now stock extremely good packs of mixed mushrooms offering an interesting selection of wild varieties which are ideal for this dish. If you choose your own, then make sure you mix for flavour (such as chanterelle), colour (try field mushrooms), and shape (for instance trumpet mushrooms). The mushrooms must, of course, be scrupulously clean to ensure that the dish is kosher.

2 shallots, finely chopped
1 clove garlic, finely chopped
100g / 3½ oz risotto rice
400g / 14 oz mixed wild mushrooms, wiped clean and sliced
250ml / 8 fl oz dry white wine
750ml / 27 fl oz vegetable stock (see page 79)
100ml / 4 fl oz olive oil
squeeze of lemon juice
chopped chives to garnish

Sweat the shallots, garlic and rice in 50ml / 3 tablespoons of the olive oil until transparent, then add half the wild mushrooms.

Add the wine and reduce until the liquid has gone. Add the vegetable stock to the rice, a ladle at a time, stirring continuously, and waiting until all the liquid has been absorbed before adding more. Do this for approximately 20 minutes, until the rice is just cooked.

While the rice is cooking, sauté the remaining mushrooms in 25ml / 1 tablespoon olive oil.

Mix the sautéed mushrooms into the risotto. Drizzle with the remaining olive oil and a squeeze of lemon juice, garnish with chopped chives, and serve.

61

❋ Chef's Tip

Be gentle and don't over-stir the mushrooms during cooking to ensure they retain their shape and texture.

Opposite: Wild Mushroom Risotto

62

Potato Gnocchi with Sorrel

Serves 4

*T*his dish does take a little effort, but you'll end up with something far superior to the pre-packed supermarket offerings – and you'll have the satisfaction of serving your guests with the genuine home-made article. One to try and practise, experimenting with shapes and sizes to suit your taste.

FOR THE GNOCCHI
800g / 1¾ lb baking potatoes
2 egg yolks
100g / 3½ oz plain flour
salt and freshly ground black pepper
≈
4 tablespoons olive oil
25g / 1 oz diced margarine
15 large sorrel leaves, finely sliced

Preheat the oven to 190C / Gas 5. Bake the potatoes for 1 hour 15 minutes until soft. Take them out of the oven and, when cool enough to handle, scoop out the potato into a bowl. (Keep the skins to use another time: deep-fry then dip in Garlic and Dill Mayonnaise, page 83.)

Add the egg yolks and flour, and mash until very smooth. Turn out onto a work surface and knead until you have an elastic dough.

Roll out the dough to a thickness of about 5mm / ¼ inch. Cut out olive-shaped pieces, then roll these with a fork to form gnocchi.

Cook the gnocchi in barely simmering water in small batches for 10 minutes. Drain well.

Toss in a hot frying pan for 2 minutes with the margarine and sorrel. Drizzle with olive oil before serving.

Opposite: Vegetable Lasagne

Vegetable Lasagne

Serves 4 - 5

FOR THE WHITE SAUCE
100g / 3½ oz margarine
100g / 3½ oz flour
1 litre / 1¾ pints soya milk
salt, pepper and 1 teaspoon English mustard to season
≈
4 red peppers
3 courgettes, thinly sliced
2 aubergines, thinly sliced
oil or margarine for frying
1 x Spicy Tomato Sauce recipe (see page 81)
200g / 7 oz lasagne sheets

63

Preheat the oven to 250C / Gas 9.

To make the white sauce, melt margarine in a pan over a medium heat, add the flour and stir until thickened. Add the milk, a little at a time, stirring continuously until all the milk has been absorbed and you have a smooth sauce. Add seasonings. Bring to the boil, turn down to simmer for 10 minutes, stirring regularly, then strain into a clean pan

Roast the peppers on a roasting tray for 10 minutes. When cool enough to handle, remove the blackened skins, de-seed and cut into slices. Reduce oven to 200C / Gas 6.

Fry the aubergine slices a few at a time in margarine or oil until golden, then drain them on kitchen paper and set them aside. Repeat the process with the courgette slices.

Place a layer of courgette, aubergine and red pepper slices on the bottom of an ovenproof dish, cover with a ladle of tomato sauce, then with a sheet of pasta, and then with a layer of white sauce. Repeat these layers until all the ingredients have been used up. Finish by covering the lasagne with white sauce.

Bake for approximately 45 minutes, checking with a skewer to ensure it has cooked thoroughly.

Pesto Tortellini

Serves 4

FOR THE PASTA DOUGH

450g / 1 lb strong flour

5 eggs

15g / ½ oz salt

2 tablespoons olive oil

≈

1 x Pesto Sauce recipe (see page 82)

150g / 5½ oz mixed salad leaves

To make the pasta, place all the ingredients for the dough in a food processor and blend until the mixture resembles fine breadcrumbs. Turn out on to a lightly-floured surface and knead until smooth. Wrap in cling film and allow to rest for 2 hours.

Using a pasta machine, roll out the dough until you reach the finest setting (or roll on a lightly-floured surface until paper-thin). Cut out the tortellini shapes using a 5cm / 2-inch cutter, or cut out circles of that diameter.

Place ½ teaspoon of pesto in the middle of each, reserving some for later. Fold the pasta over the pesto and seal with a little water. Then shape the pasta round your forefinger.

Blanch the tortellini in boiling salted water for 2 minutes.

Arrange the salad leaves in the middle of the plate and drizzle the remaining pesto over the leaves and round the edge of the plate.

Place the tortellini round the salad, and serve.

❃ *Photograph on page 67*

Making Pesto Tortellini

Mushroom Ravioli with Plum Tomatoes and Truffle Oil

Serves 4

FOR THE PASTA DOUGH
450g / 1 lb strong flour
5 eggs
15g / ½ oz salt
2 tablespoons olive oil
≈
FOR THE RAVIOLI FILLING
50g / 1¾ oz margarine
2 cloves garlic, finely chopped
400g / 14 oz mixed wild mushrooms, wiped clean and diced
50ml / 3 tablespoons vegetable stock (see page 79)
≈
800g / 1¾ lb plum tomatoes, skinned, de-seeded and halved
50ml / 3 tablespoons olive oil
1 sprig thyme
1 sprig rosemary
30ml / 1½ tablespoons white truffle oil
fresh basil and coriander to garnish

To make the pasta, place all the ingredients for the dough in a food processor and blend until the mixture resembles fine breadcrumbs. Turn out on to a lightly-floured surface and knead until smooth. Wrap in cling film and allow to rest for 2 hours.

Preheat the oven to 160C / Gas 3.

Melt the margarine in a pan and sweat the garlic and mushrooms until soft and well cooked. Moisten with the vegetable stock and cook until thick but not dry.

Place the tomatoes on a baking tray, drizzle over the olive oil and scatter with the thyme and rosemary, then bake for an hour.

Meanwhile, roll out the pasta dough on a pasta roller or a lightly-floured surface until paper-thin, then cut out ten circles per person, using a 9cm / 3½-inch round cutter.

Put a large teaspoon of the mushroom mixture in the centre of one pasta disc, moisten the edges with water, place another pasta disc on top, and then seal by crimping the edges together with your fingers. Repeat until all the pasta and mushroom mixture has been used.

Bring a large pot of salted water to the boil and blanch the ravioli for 4 minutes. Drain carefully and divide between four plates.

Dice the baked plum tomato and sprinkle over the ravioli. Drizzle with the truffle oil and serve immediately.

Garnish with fresh basil and picked coriander.

Fettuccine with Fresh Pesto and Pine Nuts

Serves 4

800g / 1¾ lb fresh fettuccine
1 x Pesto Sauce recipe (see page 82)
85g / 3 oz toasted pine nuts
1 bunch basil, leaves shredded

Cook the fettuccine according to the instructions on the packet. Drain and mix with the pesto.

Divide between four bowls, sprinkle with the toasted pine nuts and basil, and serve.

Opposite: Pesto Tortellini

66

Salads

Opposite: Oriental Smoked Chicken Salad with Sesame and Chilli Dressing, and Middle Eastern Tabouleh Salad

Oriental Smoked Chicken Salad with Sesame and Chilli Dressing

Serves 4

4 chicken breasts
vegetable oil for frying
2 tablespoons loose tea leaves
2 tablespoons brown sugar
1 teaspoon ground ginger
1 stick lemon grass, chopped
1 bunch coriander, leaves only
100g / 3½ oz mixed salad leaves
100g / 3½ oz bean sprouts
1 x Sesame and Chilli Dressing recipe (see page 84)

Line a wok with a sheet of aluminium foil, then put the tea leaves, sugar, ginger and lemon grass on top. On top of this, place a wok steamer shelf.

In a separate pan, fry the chicken breasts in a little vegetable oil for 10 minutes until almost cooked, then place on the steamer tray and cover with the wok lid.

Put the wok on a high heat until it begins to smoke, then turn the heat down very low and continue to cook for a further 10 minutes.

Slice the chicken very thinly.

Mix the coriander leaves with the bean sprouts and the mixed salad leaves. Dress with some of the sesame and chilli dressing, place the chicken on top and then drizzle over the remaining dressing.

❉ Different kinds of tea leaves such as jasmine or lapsang suchong will give their own individual flavours to the smoked chicken.
❉ A mixed continental salad leaf selection will enhance the presentation of the dish.

70

Middle Eastern Tabouleh Salad

Serves 4

A fusion of colours and flavours combine in this taste-of-the-Middle-East salad which has become a classic. Sweet vine plum tomatoes give the best flavour to this dish, which is so versatile I'd be happy to serve it with fish, as a side salad or to accompany a summer barbecue.

2 red peppers
1 aubergine
1 clove garlic
2 sprigs thyme
200g / 7 oz couscous
1 cucumber, peeled, de-seeded and diced
8 plum tomatoes, skinned, de-seeded and cut into discs
1 red onion, finely sliced
1 bunch each of basil and mint, chopped
juice of a lemon
100ml / 4 fl oz olive oil
salt and freshly ground black pepper

Preheat the oven to 250C / Gas 9, then roast the peppers, aubergine, garlic and thyme for 10 minutes. Allow to cool, then finely dice.

Mix the couscous with 400ml / 16 fl oz of cold water. Leave it to stand for 15 minutes: the couscous will only absorb as much liquid as it requires.

Mix together the couscous, vegetables and herbs, add the lemon juice and olive oil, season to taste and serve.

❉ Chef's Tip

Make an hour before serving to ensure a good blend of flavours. A great chef taught me to make the couscous with cold water to give the salad 'bite' – there's no need to cook, it still absorbs the water and doesn't go lumpy.

Salad of Chargrilled Green and White Asparagus with Roasted Red Onions

Serves 4 - 6

A sophisticated salad with the fabulous flavours of sweet red onions, concentrated through roasting and bathed in good-quality balsamic vinegar. Like a fine wine, the best balsamic can be expensive but a good bottle is worth the outlay. Something of a modern classic as a store-cupboard ingredient, it can turn the ordinary into something special.

2 bunches green asparagus (thin or wild)
2 bunches white asparagus (as thin as possible)
12 small red onions
50g / 1¾ oz brown sugar
100ml / 4 fl oz (12-year-old) balsamic vinegar
100ml / 4 fl oz olive oil
salt

Preheat the oven to 220C / Gas 7.

Peel the red onions without removing the root, cut in half, and place in a roasting tray. Sprinkle with the brown sugar and drizzle the vinegar over. Roast for 30 minutes.

Blanch the asparagus in simmering water for 2 minutes, then plunge into iced water. When completely cold, drain, then dry thoroughly.

Preheat a griddle pan until very hot.

Turn the asparagus in the olive oil, sprinkle with salt, then chargrill so that it is seared with a criss-cross pattern, taking care not to over-cook it.

To serve, place a couple of spoonfuls of roasted red onion on each plate, divide the asparagus between them, then drizzle with the juice from the onions and any remaining oil.

Salade Niçoise

Serves 4

300g / 10½ oz fresh tuna
200g / 7 oz new potatoes
200g / 7 oz green beans
2 little gem lettuces
4 plum tomatoes, skinned, de-seeded
        and quartered
4 eggs, boiled and quartered
50g / 1¾ oz anchovy fillets
20 pitted black olives
100ml / 4 fl oz olive oil
salt and freshly ground black pepper

Place the tuna under a medium preheated grill for 5 minutes each side. Allow to cool, then flake.

Boil the potatoes and, when cool enough to handle, cut them into quarters.

Cook the green beans in boiling salted water until tender, then drain thoroughly.

Separate the lettuce leaves, wash them and dry thoroughly.

Mix together all the ingredients, drizzle over the olive oil, season and serve.

✤ Keep back some tomatoes and use them to garnish the top of the salad.

71

Smoked Salmon Salad

Serves 4

After more than 20 years in banqueting, I'm still asked for this starter again and again – and why not! Typically Jewish, it is quite simply one of the all-time favourites. There are few more mouth-watering appetisers than choice smoked salmon served with mayonnaise mixed with horseradish to give it a kick.

300g / 7 oz smoked salmon
300g / 14 oz small new potatoes
2 tablespoons white horseradish (available in jars from
    supermarkets and delicatessens)
100ml / 4 fl oz mayonnaise
1 bunch chervil
1 bunch dill
4 bunches wild roquette or mixed baby leaf salad

Cook the potatoes in their skins then, while still warm, peel, cut into quarters and mix with 1 tablespoon of the horseradish and half the mayonnaise.

Just before serving, cut the smoked salmon into strips and divide between four plates. Place the salad leaves on top.

Mix the chopped herbs and potatoes with the remaining mayonnaise and horseradish and spoon them round the smoked salmon.

✳ Chef's Tip
Choose only the very best quality smoked salmon, and for a change try serving with slightly warm new potatoes to really bring out the flavour of the fish.

Caesar Salad

Serves 2

1 large cos lettuce
4 slices white bread
100ml / 4 fl oz olive oil
3 cloves garlic
100ml / 4 fl oz mayonnaise (see page 82)
55g / 2 oz anchovy fillets

Separate the lettuce leaves, wash and dry thoroughly.

Finely dice the garlic. Cut the bread into cubes and fry in the olive oil with the garlic until golden brown. Discard the garlic and drain the croûtons on kitchen paper.

Mix together the lettuce, mayonnaise, croûtons and anchovies and serve.

✳ Baby gem lettuce can be used for a slightly sweeter taste.

73

Opposite: Smoked Salmon Salad

Roasted Tomato Salad with Herbs

Serves 6

1kg / 2¼ lb vine tomatoes
1 sprig thyme
1 sprig rosemary
1 head of garlic, separated into cloves
4 shallots, sliced
250ml / 8 fl oz olive oil
1 bunch basil, chopped

Preheat the oven to 250C / Gas 9.

Wash the tomatoes, then place, together with thyme, rosemary, garlic and shallots, in a roasting tin. Pour over the olive oil and mix well, making sure that everything is thoroughly coated. Roast for 10 minutes.

Remove from the oven and leave to cool (if possible leave to marinate overnight). Serve warm, reheating in the oven if necessary, with the basil scattered over the top.

❋ Chef's Tip

Olive oil comes in various strengths and can be diluted with vegetable oils such as corn oil or sunflower oil. Save the best oils for where their flavours will stand out and best complement the food – for example, extra virgin olive oil with this tomato salad.

Artichoke, Avocado, Tomato and Roquette Salad

Serves 4

1 tin sliced artichoke bottoms, drained
2 avocados, skinned, stoned and diced
8 plum tomatoes, skinned, de-seeded and diced
8 bunches wild roquette
50ml / 3 tablespoons mayonnaise
parsley
chives

Drain the artichokes. Skin, stone and de-seed the avocados. Skin the plum tomatoes, then de-seed and dice them.

Mix together all the ingredients except the parsley and chives. Serve straight away, garnished with picked parsley and coarsely chopped chives.

❋ Chef's Tip

How to skin a tomato: With a small sharp knife, remove the core of the tomato and criss-cross the other end. Plunge the tomato into boiling water for 10 seconds, then plunge it quickly into ice-cold water, and the skin will peel away easily.

74

Opposite: Roasted Tomato Salad with Herbs

Carole Sobell's

Dips, Sauces and Dressings

Humous

Makes 1 kg / 2 lb

500g / 1 lb 2 oz cooked chickpeas (available from
      supermarkets and delicatessens)
200ml / 7 fl oz olive oil
125g / 4½ oz tahini paste
juice of 4 lemons
5 teaspoons ground cumin
8 cloves garlic
salt and freshly ground black pepper

Skin the garlic and pan-fry it in hot oil for a few minutes
until browned. Place all the ingredients in a food processor
and blend until very smooth.

    May be kept in the refrigerator for up to five days.

Guacamole

Serves 4 - 6

2 ripe avocados, skinned, stoned and finely diced
juice of 1 lime
2 shallots, finely chopped
1 green chilli, finely chopped
1 clove garlic, finely chopped
2 plum tomatoes, skinned, de-seeded and finely chopped
1 tablespoon chopped coriander
salt and freshly ground black pepper

Bind all the ingredients by mixing them together and
season to taste. Eat within a couple of hours, or the
avocado will discolour.

Salsa

Serves 4 - 6

2 red onions, finely chopped
2 red peppers, finely chopped
2 green chillies, finely chopped
1 clove garlic, finely chopped
1 plum tomato, skinned, de-seeded and finely chopped
3 sprigs coriander, shredded
1 tablespoon olive oil
juice of 2 limes
8g / ¼ oz salt

Mix together all ingredients. Keep in fridge until required.

Apple and Mustard Chutney

Makes 500g / 1 lb

10 Granny Smith apples
4 tablespoons mustard seeds
250ml / 8 fl oz white wine vinegar
225g / 8 oz caster sugar
2 onions, finely chopped
15ml / 1 tablespoon vegetable oil
zest and juice of 1 lemon
salt and freshly ground black pepper

Sauté the onions in an uncovered frying pan in the oil for
a few minutes, stirring constantly. Peel, core and chop the
apples roughly. Place all the ingredients into a large lidded
pan and cook gently for 1½ hours until all the excess
moisture is reduced. Stir throughout the cooking process.

    Add seasoning to taste. Put into sterilised jars and seal.
Keep in the refrigerator until needed – up to a month.

Vegetable Stock (Nage)

Makes approx 2 litres
(3½ pints / 70 fl oz)

100ml / 4 fl oz olive oil

250g / 8½ oz carrots, finely sliced

250g / 8½ oz celery, finely sliced

250g / 8½ oz leeks, finely sliced

250g / 8½ oz onion, finely sliced

1 fennel bulb, finely sliced

1 head of garlic, separated into cloves

1 bunch dill, roughly chopped

1 bunch parsley, roughly chopped

½ bunch tarragon, roughly chopped

100ml / 4 fl oz olive oil

2 bay leaves

20 black peppercorns

50ml / 3 tablespoons white wine vinegar

In a large pan, gently sweat the vegetables and herbs in the olive oil until tender – about 10 minutes.

Cover with 4 litres / 7 pints of water, add the bay leaves, peppercorns and vinegar, bring to the boil and simmer for 5 minutes. Leave to stand overnight.

Strain through a fine sieve and store in the refrigerator for up to four days or in the freezer for up to a month.

Fish Stock

Makes approx 2 litres
(3½ pints / 70 fl oz)

2kg / 4½ lb chopped fish bones (such as sole, turbot)

100g / 3½ oz carrots, chopped

200g / 7 oz celery, chopped

200g / 7 oz onions, choppped

200g / 7 oz leeks, sliced

1 head of garlic, separated into cloves

oil or margarine

250ml / 10 fl oz dry white wine

1 bunch dill, chopped

1 bunch parsley, chopped

1 bay leaf

3 white peppercorns

1 lemon, sliced

79

Wash the fish bones in cold water, then soak in cold water for 2 hours.

In a large lidded pan, sweat the carrots, celery, onion, leek and garlic in a little oil or margarine until soft but not coloured. Add the white wine and reduce away the liquid for about seven minutes.

Add the fish bones, herbs, peppercorns and lemon. Cover with cold water and bring to the boil, then simmer for 25 minutes, skimming continuously with a ladle. Strain through a fine sieve.

The fish stock will keep for two days in the refrigerator. Alternatively, freeze and use within one month.

Chicken Stock

Makes approx 2 litres
(3½ pints / 70 fl oz)

250ml / 10 fl oz dry white wine
2kg / 4½ lb koshered chopped chicken bones
250g / 8½ oz carrots, chopped
250g / 8½ oz onion, chopped
250g / 8½ oz leeks, sliced
250g / 8½ oz celery, chopped
1 head of garlic, separated into cloves
1 bunch parsley, chopped
1 bay leaf
3 white peppercorns

Put the wine in a large pan and cook until it has reduced by three-quarters, so that the alcohol is evaporated.

Add all the other ingredients, cover with cold water, bring to the boil then reduce heat to simmer for 2½ hours, skimming continuously with a ladle.

Strain through a fine sieve.

The stock will keep for two days in the refrigerator, or for a month in the freezer.

✳ For a fuller flavour, you can make a *brown chicken stock* by first browning the bones and vegetables in a very hot oven – 250C / Gas 9 – for 30 minutes.

Lamb Stock

Makes approx 2 litres
(3½ pints / 70 fl oz)

2kg / 4½ lb koshered lamb bones
250g / 8½ oz leeks, washed
250g / 8½ oz celery, washed
1 onion
250g / 8½ oz carrots
2 teaspoons tomato purée
1 bay leaf
10 peppercorns
4 sprigs of parsley
2 sprigs of thyme
1 sprig of rosemary

Preheat the oven to 250 C / Gas 9. Roughly chop all the vegetables and place them with the bones on a roasting tin. Put into the oven for 20-30 minutes to brown slightly.

Drain off excess oil.

Place all the ingredients in a large lidded stock pot, cover with cold water, bring to the boil, then simmer for 4-6 hours, regularly skimming off any floating residue.

Sieve and refrigerate and use within 3 days.

Beef Stock

Makes approx 2 litres
(3½ pints / 70 fl oz)

2.5kg / 5 lb koshered beef marrow bones
250g / 9 oz onion, roughly chopped
125g / 4 oz celery, roughly chopped
125g / 4 oz leeks, roughly chopped
125g / 4 oz carrots, roughly chopped
1 head of garlic, separated into cloves
1 small bunch parsley, roughly chopped
3 bay leaves
20 black peppercorns

Preheat the oven to 200C / Gas 6, then roast the beef bones for 40 minutes or until dark brown.

Brown the onion, celery, leeks, carrot and garlic for 10 minutes in a large pan with a little of the fat from the roasted beef bones.

Add the parsley, bay leaves, peppercorns and beef bones to the browned vegetables. Cover with cold water, bring to the boil and and simmer for 6 hours, topping up with cold water if necessary.

Strain through a fine sieve and store in the refrigerator for up to four days or freeze for up to two months.

❊ Venison or game bones can be used in a similar way.

Spicy Tomato Sauce

Makes approx 1 litre
(1¾ pints / 35 fl oz)

4 cloves garlic, finely chopped
4 shallots, finely chopped
50ml / 3 tablespoons olive oil
2kg / 4½ lb very ripe plum tomatoes, skinned, de-seeded and cut into quarters
4 mild medium (green) chillies, de-seeded and finely chopped
salt and freshly ground black pepper
½ bunch basil, finely chopped
½ bunch coriander, finely chopped
1 teaspoon cornflour

In a saucepan, gently cook the garlic and shallots in the olive oil for 5-10 minutes until transparent.

Add the tomatoes and 75ml / 5 tablespoons of water. Cook gently for 30 minutes on a moderate heat. Then add the chillies.

Allow to cool slightly, then liquidise until smooth.

Add salt and pepper to taste, return to the boil and adjust consistency by stirring in cornflour mixed with a little cold water.

Just before serving add the chopped herbs.

Pesto Sauce

Makes 500ml / 1 pint

2 large bunches basil
100g / 3½ oz pine nuts
2 cloves garlic, chopped
300ml / ½ pint olive oil

Place the basil, pine nuts and garlic along with all but 25ml / 1 tablespoon of the olive oil in a food processor and blend until very smooth.

Put into clean airtight jars and pour over the remaining olive oil to prevent air getting to the pesto. Store in the fridge – it will keep for 2-3 weeks.

❋ Coriander or a mix of herbs of your choice can be used instead of basil.

Mayonnaise

Makes 350ml / ¾ pint

250ml / ½ pint vegetable oil
10ml / 2 teaspoons white wine vinegar
2 egg yolks
5ml / 1 teaspoon Dijon mustard
salt and freshly ground pepper

Whisk the egg yolks, vinegar and mustard in a stainless steel or glass bowl for a couple of minutes until it emulsifies into a smooth consistency. Slowly add the olive oil in a continuous stream while continuing to whisk. Once all the oil is used, it should be the correct consistency. If it's too thick, use a little cold water to thin it down. Add seasoning to taste.

Red Wine and Shallot Sauce

Makes 400ml / ²/₃ pint

15 large shallots, finely chopped
4 cloves garlic, finely chopped
2 bottles full-bodied red wine
1 x brown chicken stock recipe (see page 80)
1 bunch thyme
75ml / 4 tablespoons ruby port
1 teaspoon cornflour, if required

Heat the shallots, garlic and red wine in a large pan and reduce until you have only 300ml / ½ pint of liquid remaining.

Add the brown chicken stock and thyme, and reduce until you have 400ml / ⅔ pint of liquid remaining or until syrupy.

Just before serving add the ruby port, but do not boil.

❋ This sauce can accompany all manner of dishes, from roast beef to fish.

❋ Cornflour can be used to aid thickening – mix it with a little cold water first.

Spicy Peanut Sauce

Makes 700ml / 1 ¹/₃ pints

400g / 14 oz roasted peanuts
200g / 7 oz margarine
30ml / 1½ tablespoons soy sauce
50ml / 3 tablespoons sesame oil
30ml / 1½ tablespoons mild chilli sauce (available from
   supermarkets and delicatessens)
40ml / 2 tablespoons runny honey
1 bunch coriander, finely chopped

Place the peanuts in a food processor and blend for
5 minutes until you have a very smooth paste.

Add the rest of the ingredients, apart from the
coriander, and blend again until smooth.

Just before serving, add the coriander.

Tartare Sauce

Makes 350ml / ³/₄ pint

350ml / ¾ pint mayonnaise (see recipe opposite)
25g / 1 oz capers, chopped
50g / 2 oz gherkins, chopped
25g / 1 oz fresh chopped parsley
salt and white pepper

Make the mayonnaise as opposite. Mix in the other
ingredients. Season to taste.

Garlic and Dill Mayonnaise

Makes 350ml / ³/₄ pint

350ml / ¾ pint mayonnaise (see opposite)
2 cloves garlic, crushed
1 bunch dill, finely chopped
1 dash Tabasco sauce

Make the mayonnaise. Mix in the other ingredients.
Season to taste.

Sweet Chilli Dipping Sauce

Serves 6

200ml / ½ pint rice wine vinegar
100g / 4 oz caster sugar
25g / 1 oz fresh root ginger
4 bird's-eye chillis (small red chillis), finely diced
½ medium cucumber, finely diced
½ red pepper, finely diced
1 clove garlic, crushed
1 shallot, finely chopped

In a saucepan, bring to the boil the vinegar, sugar, and
ginger. Reduce by half. (Avoid over-cooking as this will
caramelise the sugar.)

Remove from the heat and, while still hot, add the rest
of the ingredients.

Leave to cool so that the flavours infuse before serving.

83

Saffron and Chive Dressing

Makes 500ml / 1 pint

2g / pinch saffron
100ml / 4 fl oz white wine vinegar
salt and freshly ground black pepper
400ml / 14 fl oz olive oil
2 bunches chives

Warm the saffron with the vinegar, and a seasoning of salt and pepper, in a pan, but do not allow to boil. Remove from heat and leave to steep for 10 minutes.

When cool, add the olive oil.

Just before serving, finely chop the chives, add to the dressing, whisk thoroughly and serve.

Sesame and Chilli Dressing

Makes 500ml / 1 pint

50g / 1¾ oz white sesame seeds
50g / 1¾ oz black sesame seeds
3 green chillies, de-seeded and diced
3 red chillies, de-seeded and diced
500ml / 16 fl oz sesame oil
1 bunch coriander, chopped

Toast the sesame seeds under a preheated hot grill until golden.

Mix together the sesame seeds, chillies and sesame oil and leave for two days.

Before using the oil, add the chopped coriander.

Dijon and Balsamic Dressing

Makes 500ml / 1 pint

4 large shallots, finely chopped
4 tablespoons Dijon mustard
100ml / 4 fl oz balsamic vinegar
2 sprigs thyme
200ml / 7 fl oz olive oil
200ml / 7 fl oz ground nut oil

Mix together the shallots, mustard, balsamic vinegar and thyme leaves and add 100ml / 4 fl oz boiling water.

Pour a steady slow stream of the oils into the mustard mixture, whisking continuously, until you have a dressing that resembles runny mayonnaise.

Before serving, re-whisk to emulsify.

Thyme-flavoured Olive Oil

Makes 500ml / 1 pint

100g / 3½ oz rock salt
12 cloves garlic
6 small shallots
2 sprigs thyme
500ml / 16 fl oz olive oil

Preheat the oven to 150C / Gas 2.

Sprinkle the rock salt on a baking tray then place the garlic and shallots on top with the sprigs of thyme. Bake for 45 minutes until soft to the touch.

While the garlic and shallots are still warm, place the shallots, garlic and thyme into a jar or bottle and pour the olive oil over.

84

Balsamic Vinaigrette Dressing

Makes 500ml / 1 pint

100ml / 4 fl oz balsamic vinegar
4 tablespoons whole-grain mustard
2 tablespoons dried herbes de Provence
400ml / 14 fl oz ground nut oil

Whisk together all the ingredients. Mix well before using.

Lime and Ginger Dressing

Makes 500ml / 1 pint

zest and juice of 4 limes
25g / 1 oz fresh ginger, grated
5g / 1 teaspoon salt
100ml / 4 fl oz rice wine vinegar
200ml / 7 fl oz ground nut oil
200ml / 7 fl oz sesame oil

Add the grated ginger, lime zest, lime juice and salt to the rice wine vinegar.

Whisk the oils into the vinegar.

Carole Sobell's

Fish

Opposite: Sea Bass with Ratatouille and Tapenade Sauce

Sea Bass and Salmon en Croûte

Serves 4

400g / 14 oz sea bass fillet, thinly sliced
400g / 14 oz salmon fillet, thinly sliced
1kg / 2¼ lb puff pastry
4 shallots, finely chopped
2 cloves garlic, finely chopped
200g / 7 oz mushrooms, finely chopped
100ml / 4 fl oz vegetable stock (see page 79)
250g / 8½ oz spinach
2 eggs

Preheat the oven to 220C / Gas 7.

Place the shallots, garlic and mushrooms in a pan with the vegetable stock and cook slowly for 20 minutes until it thickens (this mixture is known as a duxelles).

Blanch the spinach for 1 minute in a pan of boiling salted water, drain, dry with a clean cloth and chop.

Roll out the puff pastry to a thickness of 2mm / ⅛ inch.

Smooth half the mushroom duxelles over the pastry, to the width of a slice of fish. Cover with a layer of sea bass, then chopped spinach, followed by salmon, and repeat these three layers until all the fish and spinach have been used. Smooth the remaining duxelles of mushroom on top.

Fold the pastry over the filling, seal the edges with a little water, and trim the edges. On a baking tray, bake in the oven for about 40 minutes until the pastry is golden.

Serve with seasoned vegetables and new potatoes.

✳ *Photograph on page 86*

88

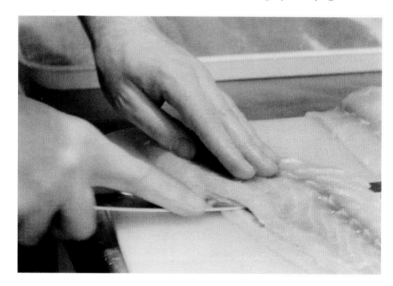

89

Sea Bass with Ratatouille and Tapenade Sauce

Serves 4

A contemporary main course you could expect to find on a sophisticated restaurant menu, this dish makes a superb and substantial alternative to a meat main course. The addition of tapenade sauce takes the sea bass to a new taste level.

4 x 150g / 5½ oz sea bass fillets
110g / 4 oz spinach (choose thick stocks)

≈

FOR THE TAPENADE SAUCE
50g / 1¾ oz margarine
100g / 3½ oz pitted black olives
40g / 1½ oz fresh anchovies
2 cloves garlic
20g / ¾ oz capers
50g / 1¾ oz flour
500ml / 16 fl oz soya milk

≈

FOR THE RATATOUILLE
3-4 tablespoons olive oil
1 red onion, chopped
2 cloves garlic, chopped
4 red peppers, de-seeded and diced
1 aubergine, diced
8 plum tomatoes, skinned and diced
2 courgettes, diced
salt and freshly ground black pepper
4 tablespoons tomato paste (purée)

Make the tapenade sauce by melting the margarine in a pan, add the olives, anchovies, capers and garlic, and sweat for 5-10 minutes until soft.

Add the flour, and a ladle of cold milk, and mix well. Continue adding the milk, a ladle at a time, stirring constantly, until it has all been absorbed, ensuring that the sauce comes to the boil each time before adding more. Allow to cool slightly, then liquidise and pass through a sieve. Keep warm.

To make the ratatouille, heat the olive oil in a pan, add the onion and garlic and sweat until soft. Add the pepper, aubergine, tomato and courgette, season with salt and pepper, and cook for about 10 minutes, then add the tomato paste. Continue cooking for a further 5 minutes, taste and adjust the seasoning.

Heat a little oil or margarine in a large pan. Season the sea bass and then fry for 3 minutes on each side.

Place the spinach in boiling salted water for 1 minute. refresh in cold water. Drain and squeeze out excess liquid. Season with salt and pepper. Mould into cylindrical shapes, one per plate. If desired, reheat in the microwave, covered, for 1 minute.

Place the fish on top of the spinach on the plate with a spoonful of ratatouille beside it.

Reheat the tapenade sauce until boiling, then spoon it around the bass and serve.

Opposite: Sea Bass with Ratatouille and Tapenade Sauce

Halibut with a Potato Crust and Truffled Mash and Spinach

Serves 4

4 x 100g / 3½ oz halibut portions
750g / 1 lb 11 oz Jersey Royal potatoes
75ml / 4 tablespoons truffle oil
1 truffle, grated
100ml / 4 fl oz olive oil
1kg / 2¼ lb fresh spinach
salt and freshly ground black pepper
squeeze of lemon

Scrape the skins of two of the Jersey Royal potatoes and slice thinly. Arrange these slices on top of each halibut portion so they look like fish scales (see Tip below).

Scrape the remaining potatoes. Cook in boiling salted water until tender, then drain well. Add the truffle oil, 50ml / 3 tablespoons olive oil and grated truffle, and mash.

Heat 25ml / 1 tablespoon olive oil in a large lidded pan. Sauté the spinach leaves over a low heat for 1 minute until wilted, then season with salt and pepper. Keep warm.

Heat the remaining olive oil in a large pan. Season the halibut and fry it, potato side down, over a medium heat for 3 minutes, until golden and crisp, then turn carefully and cook for a further 5 minutes. Add a squeeze of lemon.

Spoon the mashed potato onto warm plates, top it with the spinach, then place the halibut on top, and serve.

❊ Chef's Tip

How to stick the 'scales' to the fish:
Dry the flesh of the halibut with kitchen paper. Brush with egg yolk. Apply the scales. Re-brush with egg yolk.
❊ *If you prefer, you can flavour the mash with garlic.*

Baked Sea Bass with Tabouleh Salad

Serves 4

4 x 500g / 1 lb 2 oz sea bass, gutted and cleaned
1 onion, finely sliced
1 fennel, finely sliced
1 lemon, finely sliced
1 bunch thyme, chopped
1 bunch dill, chopped
salt and freshly ground black pepper
100ml / 4 fl oz fish stock (available in supermarkets and
 delis, or see page 79)
1 x Tabouleh Salad recipe (see page 70)

Preheat the oven to 190C / Gas 5.

If your fishmonger hasn't already done so for you, scale and gut the sea bass, remove the fins, gills and eyes, then wash well.

Mix together the vegetables and herbs and place half on a baking sheet.

Slash the flesh of the sea bass with a sharp knife. Fill these 'pockets' with some of the remaining herb and vegetable mix, then place the fish on top of the herb and vegetable mix on the baking sheet and put the rest of the herbs and vegetables on top of the fish. Baste with fish stock and season well.

Bake for 30 minutes, checking with a skewer that the middle is hot. If not, return it to the oven for 5-10 minutes.

Serve with the tabouleh salad.

Opposite: Halibut with a Potato Crust

92

Roasted Cod with Baby Vegetables and Pesto Mash

Serves 4

4 x 100g / 3½ oz cod portions
12 baby fennel
12 baby carrots
12 baby leeks
12 baby turnips
2 courgettes, cut into batons
200ml / 7 fl oz fish stock (available in supermarkets
        and delis, or see page 79)
100g / 3½ oz margarine
1 teaspoon chopped chervil
salt
15ml / 1 tablespoon olive oil for frying

≈

FOR THE PESTO MASH
800g / 1¾ lb potatoes
1 x Pesto Sauce recipe (see page 82)

Preheat the oven to 220C / Gas 7.

Blanch the vegetables until tender by placing in a large pan of boiling water for 5-7 minutes.

Peel and dice the potatoes. Simmer in salted water for 10 minutes, then drain and mash. Add the pesto, mix well, and keep warm.

Season the cod portions. Fry briefly on both sides to seal. Place in preheated oven in suitable pan and roast for 10 minutes.

Bring the fish stock to the boil, then add the blanched vegetables, chervil, margarine and a pinch of salt. Leave for 30 seconds.

Put some of the mash on a plate, place the roasted cod on top, and spoon the vegetables and their cooking juices around it.

Individual Fish Pie

Serves 4

200g / 7 oz cod fillet
200g / 7 oz salmon fillet
800g / 1¾ lb potatoes
1 tablespoon chopped chives
1 tablespoon chopped dill

≈

FOR THE WHITE SAUCE
50g / 1¾ oz margarine
50g / 1¾ oz plain flour
400ml / 14 fl oz soya milk
salt and pepper

Preheat the oven to 190C / Gas 5.

Peel and dice the potatoes. Simmer in salted water for 20 minutes, then drain and mash.

Cook the fish under a preheated medium grill for 5 minutes on each side.

Melt the margarine in a pan, add the flour and stir over a low heat for 5 minutes until cooked.

Add the milk, a little at a time, bringing the sauce to the boil each time before adding more. When all the milk has been added, season with salt and pepper, and simmer for 10 minutes, stirring occasionally. Allow to cool.

Cut the fish into chunks and mix it with the white sauce and herbs. Divide between four small ovenproof dishes.

Pipe the mashed potato on top, or smooth over with the back of a fork, then bake for 30 minutes until golden.

Opposite: Roasted Cod with Baby Vegetables and Pesto Mash

NEW JEWISH CUISINE

Seared Tuna with Roquette and a Lime and Ginger Dressing

Serves 4

A modern-day classic and an appealing alternative to the more traditional choice of salmon, tuna is now seen on every restaurant menu. Meaty enough to tempt even confirmed carnivores, yet with a nice clean taste of the Mediterranean, here it is brought bang up-to-date with the zingy dressing of lime and ginger.

200g / 7 oz new potatoes
1 x Lime and Ginger Dressing recipe (see page 85)
4 x 100g / 3½ oz tuna steaks
10ml / 1 tablespoon oil
4 x bunches wild roquette

Boil the new potatoes in salted water for 20 minutes until cooked but firm, then cut them in half lengthways. Heat the oil in a griddle pan until very hot, then chargrill the potatoes, searing the cut surfaces with a criss-cross pattern. Place in a bowl and drizzle over a little of the dressing.

Make criss-cross cuts on the tuna steaks and chargrill quickly on both sides, leaving them pink in the middle.

Mix the roquette with the potatoes and some more of the dressing. Season. Divide between four large plates, place the tuna steaks on top and drizzle over a little more of the dressing.

❊ Chef's Tip

Buy your tuna from a quality fishmonger, ask for blue fin – a dark purple in colour with a strong texture – and cook the same day. Don't be tempted to use frozen, it holds too much water and breaks down in cooking.

96

Salmon Fish Cakes with Roquette and Pesto

Serves 6

450g / 1 lb salmon fillet
350g / 12 oz potatoes
1 bunch chives, chopped
1 bunch dill, chopped
1 bunch parsley, chopped
≈
4 tablespoons seasoned flour
2 eggs, beaten
200g / 7 oz breadcrumbs
≈
4 bunches wild roquette, washed and dried
1 x Pesto Sauce recipe (see page 82)

Peel and dice the potatoes. Simmer in salted water for 20 minutes, then drain and mash.

Cook the salmon under a preheated medium grill for 5 minutes on each side. Cool and flake.

Mix together the salmon, mashed potato and herbs, roll into lime-sized balls, flatten, and chill in the refrigerator for an hour.

When the fish cakes have chilled, roll them in the flour, dip in the beaten egg, and then coat with the breadcrumbs, trying not to alter their shape. Chill for a further 30 minutes, then coat again in breadcrumbs.

Heat a deep fryer to 180C and fry the fish cakes until golden, about 4-5 minutes.

Serve the fish cakes with the roquette dressed in pesto.

❊ You can chill the fish cakes quickly by putting them in the freezer for 15 minutes, but make sure they don't start to freeze.

Assiette of Salmon — Teriyaki, Smoked & Gravadlax — with Oriental Salad

Serves 4

Sounds complicated, but couldn't be simpler. This trio of flavoured salmon served with a side salad straight from the Orient will keep the traditionalists happy yet still appeal to the more adventurous guest. It is a superb mix of flavours, quickly and easily assembled ready for serving.

100g / 3½ oz smoked
    salmon, thinly sliced
100g / 3½ oz gravadlax,
    thinly sliced
    (see page 19)
1 bunch wild roquette
1 bunch coriander
1 bunch dill
4 heads baby bok choi
    (from supermarkets
    and Chinese
    delicatessens)
1 x Sesame and Chilli
    Dressing recipe
    (see page 84)
≈

✳ Chef's Tip

Prepare the teriyaki salmon and gravadlax a day before serving so the salmon absorbs the flavour of the marinades.

FOR THE TERIYAKI SALMON
4 x 50g / 2 oz salmon fillets, with their skin on
100ml / 4 fl oz teriyaki sauce (available from supermarkets
    and delicatessens)

To make the teriyaki salmon, place the salmon in a bowl with the teriyaki sauce and marinate for 4-6 hours. Preheat the oven to 200C / Gas 6 and bake the salmon, on a baking tray, for 20 minutes. Then leave it to cool.

Dress the salad and herbs with some of the sesame and chilli dressing, then arrange in the centre of four plates.

Arrange the slices of smoked salmon, gravadlax and teriyaki salmon around the salad leaves and drizzle with some more of the dressing.

Dressed Salmon with Cucumber

Serves 8-10

1 x 4kg / 9 lb salmon, gutted and cleaned
1 large cucumber
150g / 5oz mayonnaise
≈

FOR THE COURT BOUILLON
20g / ¾ oz salt
100g / 3½ oz carrots
3 bay leaves and 4 parsley stalks
100ml / 4 fl oz vinegar
20 white peppercorns
100g / 3½ oz onion

Place all the ingredients for the court bouillon in a large pot, add 4 litres / 7 pints water, bring to the boil, simmer for 40 minutes, then strain into a clean pan.

If your fishmonger hasn't already done so, scale and remove the fins, eyes and gills from the salmon. Wash well.

Place salmon in the court bouillon, bring to a boil and simmer for 15 minutes. Turn off heat and leave the fish to cool in the court bouillon. When cool, lift out the salmon and carefully remove the skin and brown meat under the skin.

Slice the cucumber very thinly. Coat the salmon with a thin layer of mayonnaise and place one on a large salver. Arrange cucumber slices on the fish as if they were scales. Serve with mixed salad leaves, new potatoes and mayonnaise.

97

Carole Sobell's

Meat and Poultry

Opposite: Roast Rack of Lamb with Pommes Anna

Honey and Mustard Roasted Poussin with Root Vegetables

Serves 4

2 poussins
2 small parsnips
1 swede
1 celeriac
2 large carrots
1 large sweet potato
1 large baking potato
4 tablespoons whole grain mustard
4 tablespoons runny honey
500ml / 16 fl oz brown chicken stock (see page 80)
2 tablespoons vegetable oil
a sprig of flat-leaf parsley

Preheat the oven to 220C / Gas 7.

Pour the stock into the base of the roasting tray. Rub the poussins with the mustard, drizzle over the honey and roast for 45 minutes.

Peel and chop all the vegetables into 1cm / ½-inch dice, discarding the woody core of the parsnips. Blanch the potato, carrot, celeriac and swede in boiling salted water until tender (about 3-4 minutes), drain and dry thoroughly. Add the parsnip and sweet potato, then sauté in the vegetable oil for 10 minutes. They are now ready to serve and can be kept in a warm place. Add the parsley, roughly chopped, just before serving.

After the poussins have been roasting for 45 minutes, check that they are cooked by lifting them up with tongs. If the juices don't run clear, return to the oven for a further 10 minutes. If the juices run clear, the poussins are cooked, in which case leave them to rest in a warm place wrapped in aluminium foil on a wire rack.

In the roasting tray, skim the fat then reduce the cooking liquid over the heat until you are left with about 250ml / 8fl oz. Sieve and keep warm.

Serve a breast, a leg and a thigh per person, with the vegetables and some of the sauce.

100

Opposite: Honey and Mustard Roasted Poussin with Root Vegetables

102

Thai Chicken Curry with Basmati Rice

Serves 4

1 x 1.5kg / 3½ lb chicken, jointed (8 pieces)
1 tablespoon sesame oil
200g / 7 oz basmati rice

≈

FOR THE MARINADE
4 lemon grass sticks, chopped
juice of 4 limes
6 lime leaves
4 cloves garlic, crushed
2 bunches coriander (roots on)
1 bunch basil
2 green chillies
100ml / 4 fl oz sesame seed oil
200ml / 7 fl oz creamed coconut
200ml / 7 fl oz chicken stock (see page 80)

Put all the ingredients for the green curry marinade into a food processor and blend for 5 minutes until smooth. Put in a bowl, add the chicken, making sure it is well coated with the marinade, and leave overnight in the refrigerator.

Preheat the oven to 190C / Gas 5.

Remove the chicken pieces and gently pan-fry in sesame oil in a wok or large frying pan until sealed but not coloured. Then put the chicken and the marinade into an ovenproof dish and bake for 2½ hours, turning the chicken in the sauce every 15 minutes.

Just before the chicken is cooked, cook the basmati rice in 1½ litres / 2½ pints boiling salted water for 12 minutes, drain and serve with the chicken.

Opposite: Thai Chicken Curry with Basmati Rice

Poached Chicken Supreme with Lemon Grass and Sorrel Velouté

Serves 4

4 chicken supremes (breasts), with wings attached
1 litre / 1¾ pints chicken stock (see page 80)
4 sticks lemon grass
20 large sorrel leaves
150g / 5½ oz basmati rice
500g / 1 lb 2 oz spinach, washed and stalks removed
75g / 2¾ oz margarine
50g / 1¾ oz flour

Rinse rice twice in cold water to remove excess starch and prevent it sticking together, then cook in 2 litres / 3½ pints salted water for 12 minutes. Drain and cool.

Cook the spinach in boiling salted water for 1 minute, drain, plunge into iced water and drain again.

Bring the chicken stock to the boil, turn down to simmer, add the lemon grass, half the sorrel leaves and the chicken, and poach for 15 minutes. The stock should just cover the chicken breast. Remove the chicken, keep warm, and boil the poaching liquid until it is reduced by half.

Melt 50g / 1¾ oz of margarine in a pan, add the flour and cook for a minute or so. Gradually add the poaching liquid, stirring continuously, until you have a smooth sauce. Cook for 5 minutes, then strain the velouté through a fine sieve.

Toss the spinach with 25g / 1 oz of margarine in a hot wok or frying pan. Drop the rice into boiling water to reheat, then drain.

Divide the spinach and rice evenly between four plates and place the chicken supremes on top of the spinach.

Finely slice the remaining sorrel and add to the velouté. Pour it over the chicken supremes and serve.

103

Confit of Duck with Parsnips and Sweet Potatoes

Serves 4

This robust, rustic-style dish is full of wonderful flavour and should satisfy even the heartiest appetite. It is a classic peasant meal which can be made days in advance, leaving the duck in the fat, and is best enjoyed with granary bread, a rich burgundy and plenty of time to relax afterwards!

4 large duck legs
1.5 litres / 2½ pints duck fat (available at your butcher)
400g / 14 oz sweet potatoes, cut into long wedges
400g / 14 oz parsnips, cut into long wedges
2 tablespoons runny honey
4 bunches wild roquette
1 x Red Wine and Shallot Sauce recipe (see page 82)

≈

SALTING INGREDIENTS
250g / 8½ oz flaked sea salt
4 bay leaves
4 sprigs thyme
4 sprigs rosemary
zest of an orange
12 juniper berries

Mix together the salting ingredients, rub over the duck legs and leave overnight.

When ready to use the duck legs, wash off all the salt and herbs and dry thoroughly.

Heat the duck fat in a lidded pan, put in the duck legs and simmer for 2½ hours. Allow to cool in the fat.

Preheat the oven to 250C / Gas 9.

Take some of the duck fat and simmer the parsnips and sweet potatoes in a lidded pan for 8 minutes.

Remove the duck legs from the fat, wipe off any excess fat, put them in a roasting tin and drizzle with some of the honey. Roast in the oven for 10 minutes until crisp.

In some more of the duck fat, fry the parsnips and sweet potatoes with the remaining honey until caramelised. Warm the red wine sauce. Heap a little pile of the root vegetables at the top of the plate, then place some of the roquette at the bottom. Sit the duck confit on the salad and drizzle with the red wine and shallot sauce.

❋ Chef's Tip

The 'Confit' method was devised as a way of preserving meat before the days of refrigeration. Today it is used to intensify the flavours in the dish and is perfect for making several days in advance.

104

Opposite: Confit of Duck with Parsnips and Sweet Potatoes

Carole Sobell's

Noisettes of Lamb with Potato and Parsnip Rosti

Serves 6

500g / 1 lb 2 oz loin of lamb
200g / 7 oz potatoes
100g / 3½ oz parsnips
75g / 2½ oz margarine
50ml / 3 tablespoons olive oil
salt
500ml / 16 fl oz lamb stock (see page 80)
10 plum tomatoes, skinned, de-seeded and diced
5 sprigs thyme
4g / ⅛ oz garlic

Ask your butcher to cut the lamb into noisettes, removing all the fat and gristle, and then to flatten them a little.

Preheat the oven to 190C / Gas 5.

Grate the potatoes and parsnips, and mix with a little of the margarine and olive oil and a good pinch of salt. Add crushed garlic if required. In a large, dry, hot frying pan, fry 10cm / 4-inch rounds of the potato mixture until golden on both sides (I use a stainless steel mould to maintain their shape while frying). Then place on a baking tray and bake in the oven for 10 minutes. Drain on kitchen paper to remove any excess oil.

Meanwhile, place the lamb stock, together with the diced tomato and thyme, in a pan and simmer until it reduces down to about 200ml / 7 fl oz / ⅓ pint of liquid. Strain through a fine sieve and keep warm.

Pan-fry the lamb noisettes in a little oil or margarine for a minute on each side so that they remain pink.

Place the rosti on four separate, hot, plates. Put the noisettes on top, pour the sauce around the outside and serve.

✳ Chef's Tip

How to skin tomatoes:
With a small sharp knife,
remove the core of the tomato
and criss-cross the other end.
Plunge the tomato into
boiling water for 10 seconds,
and then plunge quickly into
ice-cold water and the skin
will peel away easily.

106

Roast Rack of Lamb with a Panache of Vegetables and Parmentier Potatoes

Serves 6

4 x 3-boned racks of lamb (French trimmed)
750g / 1 lb 11 oz potatoes, cut into 1cm / ½-inch dice
salt and freshly ground black pepper
8 sprigs rosemary
75g / 2½ oz fine beans
75g / 2½ oz baby carrots
75g / 2½ oz courgettes, cut into batons
75g / 2½ oz baby turnips
75g / 2½ oz baby leeks
75g / 2½ oz mangetout
50g / 1¾ oz parsley, chopped
500ml / 16 fl oz lamb stock (see page 80)
50g / 1¾ oz margarine

Preheat the oven to 250C / Gas 9.

Season the racks of lamb with salt and pepper.

Boil the lamb stock until it has reduced to 100ml / 4 fl oz / ¼ pint.

Wash the diced potatoes until the water runs clear. Drain and dry thoroughly.

Preheat a deep-fat frying pan to 140C and fry the potatoes for 8 minutes. Remove the potatoes from the fryer but keep the fryer on low.

Pan-fry the racks of lamb in a little oil or margarine in a very hot pan until golden all over, then put them in a roasting tin and roast for 8 minutes with the rosemary. Remove from the oven, wrap in aluminium foil and rest on a cooling rack in a warm place for 10 minutes.

Cook the beans, carrots, courgettes, turnips and leeks in boiling salted water for 5 minutes, then add the mangetout and cook for a further 2 minutes. Drain and mix with the margarine and a good pinch of salt.

While the vegetables are cooking, increase the heat in the deep-fat fryer to 180C. Return the potatoes to the fryer for 4 minutes until crisp and golden. Remove and, whilst still hot, add the parsley to the potatoes.

Divide the vegetables and potatoes between four large, hot, plates, arranging them around the outside. Slice each rack of lamb into three chops and place in the middle of the plate. Drizzle with the warm reduced sauce and serve.

107

❋ Style Tip

Scrape the lamb bones very clean before roasting and cover them with tin foil for three-quarters of the roasting time to keep them white and achieve a brilliant final presentation of the dish.

Roast Rack of Lamb with Pommes Anna

Serves 4

When you are out to impress, this stunning dish is hard to beat as it is not only delicious but looks great. The use of fresh garlic, rosemary and thyme infuses the meal with superb flavours. A dinner-party favourite which never fails to stop the show.

2 racks of lamb, 6 bones on each rack
500ml / 16 fl oz lamb stock (see page 80)
450g / 1 lb lamb fat
1 sprig thyme
1 sprig rosemary
4 cloves garlic
1 sprig thyme
750g / 1 lb 11 oz potatoes, peeled and thinly sliced
salt
4 baby fennel bulbs
4 baby carrots
100g / 3½ oz fine green beans
4 baby turnips
1kg / 2¼ lb spinach

Preheat the oven to 190C / Gas 5.

Heat the lamb stock in a pan until reduced to a syrup. Keep warm.

In another pan, simmer the lamb fat with the rosemary, garlic and thyme. Leave to cool for 10 minutes.

❋ Style Tip

Serve on a large plate and rest the lamb bones against the stack of Pommes Anna to give height and eye appeal to the dish.

Line the bottom of an ovenproof dish with greaseproof paper. Cover with a layer of potato, then spread with some of the lamb fat and a pinch of salt. Place another layer of potato on top and continue thus, ending with a layer of potato, until all the potato and lamb fat have been used. Bake in the oven for about an hour until tender. Keep warm.

Increase the oven temperature to 230C / Gas 8, then roast the lamb for 12 minutes – it should be pink.

Meanwhile, cook the fennel, carrot, green beans and turnip in boiling salted water for 5 minutes or until tender.

Return the Pommes Anna to the oven for a couple of minutes if needed.

Cook the spinach in a little water for 1 minute until wilted.

Serve the lamb with the potato and vegetables, drizzling the syrupy sauce over the lamb.

109

Opposite: Roast Rack of Lamb with Pommes Anna

Salt Beef Sandwich

Serves 6

A traditional and much-loved snack which has stood the test of time to become part of classic Jewish cuisine. Great as a light supper, here it is served in the club sandwich style and teamed with matchstick chips to give a modern feel to an old favourite. It has long been enjoyed as a 'Sunday night special' in my home. So just go for the 'wow!' factor and make it large!

200g / 7 oz salt beef, thinly sliced
1 loaf rye bread, sliced
4 plum tomatoes, sliced
250g / 8½ oz mixed salad leaves
100ml / 4 fl oz dill mayonnaise
200g / 7 oz dill pickles
100g / 3½ oz deep-fried matchstick chips (see page 26)

Fill each sandwich with five slices of the beef, some salad leaves, and slices of tomato.

Cut each sandwich diagonally in half, secure with a cocktail stick, and garnish with the mayonnaise, dill pickles and matchstick chips.

❋ Style Tip

Team the salt beef sandwich with generous bowls of crunchy coleslaw and fresh salad for a great casual supper with friends.

Opposite: Salt Beef Sandwich

Lancashire Hotpot

Serves 6

One of my all-time favourites and a dish I have served to my family again and again. It's a wonderful winter warmer and I have found it's so tasty, it's a great way of getting children to eat vegetables!

4 large lean lamb cutlets
1 tablespoon oil or margarine
2 sprigs rosemary
1 garlic clove
100g / 3½ oz leek, chopped and washed carefully
100g / 3½ oz onion, chopped
50g / 1¾ oz celery, chopped into 1cm / ½-inch dice
100g / 3½ oz carrots, chopped into 1cm / ½-inch dice
400g / 14 oz potatoes, peeled and thinly sliced
900ml / 1⅔ pints lamb stock (see page 80)

Preheat the oven to 200C / Gas 6.

Brown the chops in a little oil or margarine in a hot pan, then put in a shallow roasting tray with the rosemary. In the same pan, brown the garlic, leek, onion, celery and carrots, then sprinkle them over the lamb.

Pan-fry the potatoes until golden, then arrange them over the lamb chops, so that the potatoes are like the crust on a pie. Heat the lamb stock in the same pan and pour it over the hotpot.

Bring the hotpot in the roasting tray to the boil on top of the stove, then cook in the oven for 45 minutes.

Serve the hotpot in bowls, with good crusty bread.

111

Tsimmes with Dumplings

Serves 6

This can also serve eight as a side dish, although you can never make enough tsimmes for everyone!

A Rosh Hashanah (New Year) speciality, a tsimmes is a very rich, rustic-style stew, here sweetened with golden syrup. It rightly earns its place in classic Jewish cuisine as a recipe which everyone recalls as something Grandmother used to make. Served with the dumplings, it is a substantial special occasion meal – but note that it will be cooking for six hours!

900 g / 2 lb brisket, in a piece
1.5kg / 3½ lb carrots, peeled and cut into 1cm / ½ inch dice
4 slightly rounded tablespoons golden syrup
¼ teaspoon white pepper
2 teaspoons salt
1 tablespoon cornflour
675g / 1½ lb potatoes, peeled and cut into large cubes

≈

FOR THE DUMPLINGS (OPTIONAL)
75g / 3 oz margarine
*175 g / 6½ oz self-raising flour **or** 175g / 6½ oz plain flour*
plus 1½ teaspoons baking powder
½ teaspoon salt
3-4 tablespoons water

Trim any excess fat from the meat, leaving a thin edging, then cut it into 4cm / 1½-inch chunks. Put it in a pan with the carrots, barely cover with hot water, then add half the golden syrup, all the pepper and ½ teaspoon of salt. Bring to the boil, and simmer gently for 2 hours, either on top of the stove or in an oven preheated to 150C / Gas 2. Periodically skim off the fat or, if possible, chill overnight, so that it can be removed more easily.

Four hours before you want to serve the tsimmes, make the dumplings by rubbing the margarine into the flour and salt until you have a mixture resembling breadcrumbs. Add the water and mix to a soft dough. Mould into oval dumplings and put them in the middle of a large oval earthenware, enamel or enamelled cast-iron casserole. Lift the meat and carrots from their cooking liquid with a slotted spoon and arrange around the dumplings. (If you don't have dumplings, simply put the carrots and meat into the casserole.)

Mix the cornflour with enough water to make a smooth cream, then stir into the cooking liquid from the carrots and meat. Bring to the boil and pour over the carrots and meat.

Arrange the potatoes on top of the carrots and meat, adding extra boiling water if necessary so that they are just submerged. Sprinkle with the remaining salt and golden syrup. Cover and bring to the boil on top of the stove, then transfer to a slow oven, 150C / Gas 2, for 3½ hours.

Uncover and taste, adding a little more syrup if necessary. Return to the oven for a further half an hour, then serve. The potatoes and dumplings should be lightly browned and the sauce slightly thickened.

Opposite: Tsimmes with Dumplings

Beef Wellington

Serves 4

A great British dinner party dish, the spectacle of carving Beef Wellington at the table has been enjoyed for decades. The use of rib eye as an alternative cut to the original fillet ensures that the dish meets Jewish dietary needs and so earns its place in new Jewish cuisine. Perfect for a candle-lit, special-occasion dinner party.

1 x 1kg / 2 lb rib-eye beef
100g / 3½ oz shallots, finely chopped
8g / ¼ oz garlic, finely chopped
200g / 7 oz mushrooms, finely chopped
2 tablespoons olive oil
750g / 1 lb 11 oz puff pastry
2 egg yolks, beaten with a little salt

≈

FOR THE PANCAKE BATTER
1 egg
1 egg yolk
15ml / 3 teaspoons olive oil
250ml / 8 fl oz soya milk
75g / 2½ oz flour

≈

1 x Red Wine and Shallot Sauce recipe (see page 82)

Make the pancake batter by mixing together all ingredients, except for the flour, until smooth. Then add the flour, and stir until smooth. Pass the batter through a sieve, and allow to rest in the refrigerator for 20 minutes.

Heat a large non-stick frying pan, add a little oil or margarine, wiping it over the surface of the pan with kitchen paper, pour on a ladle of batter, tipping the pan so that it is evenly coated, and cook for a minute on both sides. Repeat until all the batter has been used, stacking

❊ Chef's Tip

Make sure that the mushrooms are well drained and the meat is well sealed before wrapping in pastry, to avoid juices seeping through.

the cooked pancakes on a plate interleaved with greaseproof paper.

In a separate large pan, brown the beef on all sides in a tablespoon of oil, then rest on a cooling rack. Gently cook the shallots, garlic and mushrooms in a tablespoon of oil until soft and any moisture has evaporated.

Roll out the puff pastry on a lightly-floured surface until you have a very thin rectangular shape of roughly the same length as the beef. Cover the pastry with the pancakes, then spread these with the mushroom mixture. The pancakes will keep the pastry crisp.

Place the fillet of beef on top, then roll up, making sure that the seam is on the bottom. Trim off any excess pastry and rest in the refrigerator for an hour or overnight.

Preheat the oven to 220C / Gas 7.

Brush the pastry with the beaten egg yolks, then bake for 45 minutes – the beef will be pink in the middle.

Cut the Beef Wellington into slices, allowing two per person.

Gently heat the red wine sauce and drizzle a little round the beef. Serve on a large serving dish, accompanied by green vegetables.

114

Traditional Roast Beef with Yorkshire Pudding and Seasonal Vegetables

Serves 6

1.2kg / 4½ lb rib of beef

200ml / 7 fl oz vegetable oil

salt and freshly ground black pepper

600ml / 21 fl oz beef stock (see page 81),
reduced to 200 ml / 7 fl oz

1.35kg / 3 lb potatoes

50g / 1¾ oz baby carrots

50g / 1¾ oz courgettes

50g / 1¾ oz fine beans

50g / 1¾ oz baby turnips

50g / 1¾ oz baby leeks

50g / 1¾ oz mangetout

50g / 1¾ oz margarine

600ml / 21 fl oz beef stock (see page 81)

≈

FOR THE YORKSHIRE PUDDING

100g / 3½ oz plain flour

2 eggs

250ml / 8 fl oz soya milk

Preheat the oven to 250C / Gas 9.

On the stove, boil the beef stock until it has reduced down to 200ml / 7 fl oz / ⅓ pint.

Make the Yorkshire pudding batter by whisking together the flour and eggs with a pinch of salt, add the milk, then strain through a sieve and allow to rest.

In a large roasting tray, heat half the vegetable oil, season the beef well, and brown on all sides on the stove.

Peel and cut the potatoes into 3cm / 1-inch squares, boil rapidly in salted water for 4 minutes, then drain and shake vigorously until the edges start to soften.

Put the potatoes round the beef and roast for 45 minutes. Remove the beef, wrap in aluminium foil and allow to rest for 20 minutes in a warm place. Reduce the oven temperature to 230C / Gas 8.

If the potatoes are not cooked, return them to the oven until they are crisp, then keep warm.

Heat the Yorkshire pudding tray, then add a little vegetable oil and fill two-thirds full with batter mixture. Bake for 5 minutes, then reduce the oven temperature to 190C / Gas 5 and bake for a further 20 minutes.

Cook the carrots, courgettes, beans, turnips and leeks in boiling salted water for 5 minutes, then add the mangetout and cook for a further 2 minutes. Drain, mix with the margarine, and keep warm.

Heat up the reduced beef stock. A little cornflour dissolved in water can be added to thicken the sauce.

Carve the beef into thin slices and serve with the roast potatoes, vegetables, Yorkshire pudding and the reduced beef sauce.

115

Desserts

Opposite: Chocolate Truffle Heart with Summer Berry Fruits and Raspberry Coulis

Chocolate Truffle Heart with Summer Berry Fruits and Raspberry Coulis

S e r v e s 4 - 6
(depending on size of mould)

This romantic dessert will melt any heart. The chocolate truffle is simply wicked, while the fresh fruit and mint freshen the palate, making it a summer afternoon delight. Note that the hearts should ideally be left in the fridge overnight... if you can keep your hands off them!

475g / 1 lb 1 oz dark bitter chocolate (70% cocoa solids)
475ml / 15½ fl oz soya cream
8g / ¼ oz cocoa powder
1 punnet fresh strawberries
1 punnet raspberries
1 punnet blueberries
1 punnet redcurrants
1 bunch fresh mint

≈

FOR THE RASPBERRY COULIS
1 punnet raspberries
8g / ¼ oz icing sugar
squeeze of lemon juice

To make the raspberry coulis, blend all the coulis ingredients in a food processor, then pass through a fine sieve.

To make the chocolate truffle hearts, melt the chocolate in a glass bowl on top of a pan of simmering water, taking care not to let it overheat.

Lightly whisk the soya cream, then fold in the chocolate, and spoon into heart-shaped moulds. Place in the refrigerator to set for at least four hours – and preferably overnight.

Using a warm knife, loosen the chocolate hearts. Dust liberally with cocoa powder and then place each in the centre of a white plate.

Garnish with strawberries cut in quarters, raspberries, blueberries and redcurrants and sprigs of fresh mint.

Drizzle raspberry coulis over the fruits.

❊ *Photograph on page 116*

118

Crêpe Suzette with Oranges and Caramel

Serves 4

*I*am always asked to include this classic on dessert buffets at banquets – and it's still as delicious as it always has been. The great thrill is to see the chef flambé the crêpes at the table – which is said to be the way it was originally served at the Café de Paris in France – but they are just as good made in advance and brought back to heat with the warmed sauce.

FOR THE CRÊPE BATTER
75g / 2½ oz flour
1 egg
1 egg yolk
20g / ¾ oz caster sugar
zest and juice of 2 tangerines
220ml / 7½ fl oz soya milk
≈
6 oranges, segmented
juice of 6 oranges (and the zest of one)
3 tablespoons brandy
1 teaspoon caster sugar
75g / 2½ oz icing sugar

Whisk together the flour, egg, egg yolk, caster sugar and tangerine juice and zest, then gradually add the milk, whisking continuously. Leave to rest for 2 hours.

Heat a non-stick frying pan, wipe over a little oil or margarine using kitchen paper, then ladle on a spoonful of batter, tipping it to ensure it is evenly coated, and cook for a minute or so each side. When done, stack the crêpes on a plate, interleaved with greaseproof paper. Keep warm. This amount of batter should make 8-10 crêpes.

Put the brandy in a pan. Light it, using a blowtorch or a match. (It will go out when the alcohol has been burned away, leaving the brandy flavour.) Add the juice of six

oranges, the zest of one and one teaspoon of caster sugar, and boil until reduced by half to make the caramel sauce.

Dust the orange segments with icing sugar, then caramelise using a blowtorch or under a preheated hot grill. Reserve resulting juices.

To serve, place a crêpe plus some of the orange segments on a plate and then drizzle over the juices and the caramel sauce and serve.

✷ Chef's Tip

If you want to flambé the crêpes, a safer alternative at home is to take a dish of hot brandy to the table and light at arm's length with a safety match – and don't forget to turn down the lights first!

119

Lockshen Kugel

Serves 6

This traditional pudding, originally made on Fridays and cooked overnight so that it could be served hot on the Sabbath, is quite heavy. To give it a lighter touch and a more modern presentation, I like to cut the long loaf into squares, drizzle with sauce and garnish with berry fruits. It can be served cold, but is much nicer hot.

The crusty lining, which is the best part of a kugel, comes from heating the margarine in the baking dish and then swirling it round the sides.

50g / 2 oz margarine
225g / 8 oz egg noodles, broad or narrow as preferred,
  but no broader than 5mm / ¼ inch
2 eggs
125g / 4½ oz caster sugar
a pinch of cinnamon
a pinch of salt
1 grated apple (cooking apple or Granny Smith)
grated zest of ½ lemon
50g / 2 oz raisins
50g / 2 oz chopped glacé fruit (optional)

Preheat the oven to the preferred temperature (see below). Put the margarine in either a 5cm / 2-inch deep oven-to-table casserole measuring about 25 x 20 cm / 10 x 8 inches or a round 18-20cm / 7-8 inch soufflé dish or 'teppel', with a liquid capacity of 1.5 litres / 2½ pints.

Put this into the oven. Meanwhile, boil the noodles

❊ Style Tip

Serve in the centre of a big plate and dust the edges with cocoa-powder if using light crockery, or icing sugar on dark plates – something of a Sobell signature!

according to the packet directions, then drain well.

Whisk the eggs and the sugar to blend, then stir in the cinnamon, salt, zest, raisins, apple and glacé fruit, if using. Stir in the noodles. Swirl the hot fat round the baking dish to coat the sides, then stir it into the mixture.

Pour into the baking dish. Bake either at 190C / Gas 5 for 45 minutes or at 150C / Gas 2 for 1½ hours. In either case it should be set inside and crisp and brown on top.

❊ The kugel can be kept for three days in the refrigerator and for up to three months in the freezer.

Opposite: Lockshen Kugel

Sticky Toffee Pudding with Caramel Sauce and Crème Anglaise

Serves 6 - 8

50g / 2 oz dates, pitted and chopped
225g / 8 oz margarine
175g / 6 oz soft brown sugar
4 eggs, lightly beaten
225g / 8 oz plain flour
1 teaspoon baking powder
1 x Crème Anglaise recipe (see page 136)
≈

FOR THE CARAMEL SAUCE
100g / 3½ oz brown sugar
100g / 3½ oz margarine
100ml / 4 fl oz soya whipping cream
100ml / 4 fl oz golden syrup

Preheat the oven to 180C / Gas 4.

Butter and flour four 5cm / 2-inch pudding moulds.

Place the dates in a pan with 150ml / 5 fl oz water, bring to the boil, simmer for 2 minutes.

Cream the margarine and brown sugar by beating together until light and fluffy.

Gradually add the dates and the eggs to the creamed mixture, then fold in the flour and baking powder.

Spoon into the greased moulds and bake for 45 minutes or until firm to the touch.

Place all the caramel sauce ingredients in a saucepan, bring to the boil and simmer for 5 minutes, whisking occasionally.

Serve warm with both the caramel sauce and some crème anglaise poured over.

Individual Chocolate Puddings

Serves 4 - 6

100g / 3½ oz margarine
150g / 5½ oz caster sugar
3 eggs
125g / 4 oz self-raising flour
¾ oz cocoa powder
100g / 3½ oz bitter chocolate (70% cocoa solids), grated

Lightly grease four 150ml / 5 fl oz pudding bowls with a little margarine.

Cream the margarine and sugar by beating together until light and fluffy.

Lightly beat the eggs. Gradually add the eggs to the creamed mixture, beating continuously as you do so.

Fold in the flour, cocoa and grated chocolate.

Spoon into the four greased pudding bowls, cover with aluminium foil and secure with string.

Place in a steamer, or in a lidded saucepan filled with water to halfway up the bowls. Bring the water to the boil, then turn down to simmer. Steam for 60 minutes, making sure it doesn't boil dry.

Turn out and serve with crème anglaise (see page 136) or vanilla ice cream (page 140).

Opposite: Sticky Toffee Pudding with Caramel Sauce and Crème Anglaise

Crème Brûlée

Serves 6

600ml / 21 fl oz soya cream
5 large eggs
½ teaspoon vanilla essence
60g / 2½ oz caster sugar

Preheat the oven to 120C / Gas ½.

Mix the cream, eggs, vanilla and half the sugar in a large bowl, then pour into a baking dish, or individual oven-proof bowls. Place the dish or bowls in a roasting tin containing hot water to a depth of 2.5cm / 1 inch, then bake in the oven for about an hour or until just firm.

Leave to cool, then refrigerate for at least 4 hours, or overnight. About ten minutes before serving, preheat a hot grill (unless you plan to use a blowtorch).

Cover the chilled cream mixture with the remaining sugar, working it through a sieve.

Brown under the grill for 3 or 4 minutes, or heat with a blowtorch for a minute, until the sugar has melted and formed a golden crust over the custard. Don't do this too early, as the sugar will become soft and lose its crispness.

Leave to cool.

❋ Chef's Tip
A small hand-held blowtorch can be obtained from hardware shops or good cookshops. It is easy and safe to use and runs on a small gas refill bottle.

Opposite: Crème Brûlée

Carole Sobell's

Roast Baby Pineapple with Vanilla Ice Cream and Chilli

Serves 4

For the 'wow!' factor, this most modern of desserts has the lot. It blends sweet and succulent pineapple with a surprising tang of chilli smoothed over with the velvety vanilla ice cream. A real treat to take the tastebuds from hot and spicy to cool and smooth, it's a guaranteed talking point to round off any dinner party. Presentation can be half the fun of cooking, and this recipe will help you to do it in style.

4 small pineapples, skinned and cored
2 vanilla pods
1 large mild red chilli
100g / 3½ oz caster sugar
50ml / 3 tablespoons rum
1 x Vanilla Ice Cream recipe (see page 140)

✳ Chef's Tip

When handling chilli, either wear gloves or wash your hands immediately afterwards, as it can cause burns and severe irritation if it comes into contact with your skin. And don't rub your eyes!

Preheat the oven to 190C / Gas 5.

To present the pineapple as in the photograph, hold the leaves firmly and twist. This will separate the leaves from the pineapple. Don't throw the leaves away! Remove the lower leaves and with a sharp knife square off the base of the bunch. Retain these for the final presentation. With a sharp knife, remove the top and bottom of the pineapple. Stand the pineapple upright on a chopping board. Shave off the peel. Score the pineapple in a spiral fashion.

Retain all the juice from the peelings to be used in the cooking process.

Cut the vanilla pods and chilli into very thin strips, discarding the chilli seeds unless you prefer a hotter dish. Stud the pineapples with the vanilla and chilli.

In a small ovenproof dish, lightly caramelise the caster sugar under a grill or using a blowtorch, then, in order to stop it over-cooking, pour in the rum.

Put the pineapples in the dish, pouring in any juice left from the peelings, and roast for 45 minutes, basting five or six times.

Serve with some of the cooking juice and a scoop of vanilla ice cream.

127

Opposite: Roast Baby Pineapple with Vanilla Ice Cream and Chilli

Carole Sobell's

Bitter Chocolate with Caramelised Walnut and Honey Delight

Serves 6

FOR THE WALNUT PRALINE
200g / 7 oz caster sugar
150g / 6 oz roasted walnuts, halved

To make the walnut praline, place the 200g / 7 oz caster sugar in a pan and heat gently until totally melted and golden brown. Stir in the walnut halves, then spread out on an oiled baking sheet to cool. When cold, blend in a food processor.

≈

FOR THE HONEY DELIGHT
50g / 2 oz caster sugar
5 egg yolks
2 tablespoons honey
250ml / 8 fl oz soya whipping cream
100g / 3½ oz bitter chocolate (70% cocoa solids), grated

To make the honey delight, place the 50g / 2 oz caster sugar in a pan with 100ml / 4 fl oz of water, bring to the boil and simmer for 3 minutes. In a mixing bowl, pour this slowly into the egg yolks, whisking continuously until stiff – about 10 minutes. Whisk the cream until it forms soft peaks. Fold in the eggs, chocolate and honey and walnut praline. Line a bread loaf tin with cling film. Pour in the mixture and freeze for a minimum of 8 hours.

FOR THE CARAMEL SPIRALS
225g / 8 oz caster sugar
teaspoon of glucose
50ml water

To make the caramel spirals, put the sugar and glucose in the water and bring to the boil until golden brown. Remove from heat. Allow to cool for 10 minutes. Place spoon in caramel. Lift out, and the sugar will form a thread. Twist the thread of sugar round the handle of a wooden spatula. When this sets, slip off to form sugar spirals.
✳ *Note:* Take care not to splash your skin; the caramel will burn.

≈

FOR THE CHOCOLATE TOWER
150g / 6 oz bitter chocolate (70% cocoa solids)
greaseproof paper

To make the chocolate tower, melt the chocolate in a glass bowl in the microwave or over hot water. Spread the melted chocolate onto the centre of a sheet of greaseproof paper. Roll the paper into a cylinder, allowing the chocolate to overlap by a few millmetres. Place in the refrigerator for 10-15 minutes. Carefully peel the greaseproof paper off the chocolate. Using a hot, dry sharp knife, trim the cylinder into six segments of about 8cm / 3 inches in length.

≈

To assemble, place the chocolate cylinder in the centre of the plate. Fill to three-quarters with scoops of Honey Delight. Arrange sugar spirals on top. Decorate the plate with melted chocolate and crème anglaise sauce (see page 136).

Opposite: Bitter Chocolate with Caramelised Walnut and Honey Delight

Carole Sobell's

129

Assiette of Poached Fruits with Mango and Raspberry Sorbets

Serves 4

500g / 1 lb 2 oz caster sugar
4 vanilla pods
4 passion fruit
2 Granny Smith apples, peeled and cored
2 firm William pears, peeled and cored
1 large mango, peeled and stoned
12 large strawberries, hulled
100g / 4 oz raspberries
2 kiwi fruit, peeled and sliced
2 peaches, peeled and halved
1 x Mango Sorbet recipe (see page 142)
1 x Raspberry Sorbet recipe (see page 142)

Place the sugar, vanilla pods and passion-fruit pulp in a large pan with 500ml / 16 fl oz water and bring to a simmer. Add the apple and pears and simmer for 3 minutes or until tender. Add the rest of the fruit and simmer for a further minute, then cool on a plastic tray, reserving the liquid.

In a stem serving glass, serve the poached fruit drizzled with some of the liquid, with the mango and raspberry sorbets.

Tarte au Citron with Seasonal Berries with Raspberry Coulis

Serves 6

1 x 22cm / 8½-inch pastry case baked blind (see page 151)
800ml / 1½ pints soya cream
110g / 4 oz caster sugar
8 large eggs
zest and juice of 6 lemons
2 punnets raspberries
1 tablespoon icing sugar
1 punnet strawberries
1 punnet redcurrants

Mix 75g / 3 oz caster sugar with the eggs, lemon juice and zest for 2 minutes. Add the soya cream. Leave to stand for 4-6 hours to intensify the flavour.

Preheat the oven to 130C / Gas ½ .

Sieve the mixture. Pour it into the pastry case and bake for approximately 1 hour until *just* set.

Allow to cool. Do not refrigerate.

To make the coulis, liquidise one of the punnets of raspberries with the icing sugar, then pass through a fine sieve.

When the tarte is cool, sprinkle with the remaining sugar, and caramelise using a blowtorch or hot grill, until the sugar bubbles and goes brown. (Do not over-cook or you may curdle the tarte, and don't touch the caramel as it will be very hot!)

Serve the tarte in slices, with some of the berries and a drizzle of the coulis.

130

Assiette Gourmande: Raspberry Sorbet, Passion Fruit Mousse, Chocolate Mousse and Lemon Tarte with Raspberry Coulis

Serves 4

A firm favourite at banquets, this delightful combination dessert isn't as complicated as it sounds. It is a little time-consuming to prepare but can be made well in advance and assembled on the day. Your efforts will be repaid in the reception it receives, as it looks great and offers something for everyone.

4 slices Tarte au Citron (see opposite)

12 tuile baskets (see Plain Tuiles recipe, page 146)

seasonal berries to garnish

1 bunch mint to garnish

≈

FOR THE RASPBERRY SORBET

5 punnets raspberries

75g / 2½ oz icing sugar

juice of a lemon

≈

FOR THE CHOCOLATE MOUSSE

100g / 4 oz bitter chocolate (70% cocoa solids)

125ml / 3 fl oz whipping soya cream

≈

FOR THE PASSION FRUIT MOUSSE

½ Pastry Cream recipe (see below)

pulp of 4 passion fruit

50ml / 2 fl oz whipping soya cream

≈

FOR THE PASTRY CREAM (MAKES 300ML / ½ PINT)

½ split vanilla pod

3 egg yolks

50g / 2 oz caster sugar

20g / ¾ oz plain flour

250ml / 8 fl oz soya milk

pulp of 4 passion fruit

4 tuile baskets (see Plain Tuiles recipe, page 146)

To make the pastry cream, heat the milk with the vanilla pod. Do not boil. In a mixing bowl, stir the eggs with the sugar for 5 minutes. Add the flour and mix again. Pour hot milk into the egg mixture in a steady stream, stirring continuously. Pour the mixture into a clean pan, return to the stove, and stir for 1 minute. Do not boil. Remove and cover with cling film so that it does not form a skin. Pastry cream can be used as a base for fruit tartlets or to fill profiteroles.

To make the raspberry sorbet, liquidise the raspberries with the icing sugar and lemon juice, pass through a fine sieve, and churn all but 30ml / 1 fl oz in an ice cream machine for 15 minutes until firm, then freeze. Chill the reserved coulis.

To make the chocolate mousse, melt the chocolate in a glass bowl, either in the microwave or over hot water. Add in half the whipping cream. Whisk remaining cream to stiff peaks. Fold together. Refrigerate for at least 2 hours.

To make the passion fruit mousse, whip the cream then bind together with the pastry cream and passion fruit pulp to form a light mousse.

On a large white plate, put a small slice of tarte au citron. Place three tuile baskets round the edge of the plate.

Fill one tuile with piped chocolate mousse, another with piped passion fruit mousse, and fill the remaining tuile with sorbet.

Dust with icing sugar, drizzle with raspberry coulis, and garnish with fresh seasonal berries and mint.

131

Summer Pudding with an Apple Sorbet and Raspberry Coulis

Serves 4

3 punnets raspberries
50g / 1¾ oz caster sugar
½ loaf white bread, thinly sliced
1 punnet strawberries
1 punnet blackberries
1 punnet redcurrants
1 punnet blueberries
1 punnet blackcurrants
1 teaspoon of lemon juice

≈

FOR THE APPLE SORBET
8 Granny Smith apples, peeled and cored
100g / 3½ oz icing sugar
juice of a lemon

To make the apple sorbet, place the apples in a liquidiser with the sugar, lemon juice and 100ml / 4 fl oz water. Blend, then pass through a fine sieve. Churn in an ice-cream machine for 15 minutes until firm, then freeze.

Liquidise two of the punnets of raspberries with the caster sugar, then pass through a sieve to make the coulis.

Line four 150ml / 5 fl oz moulds with cling film. Dip the bread in the coulis and use to line the moulds, reserving four slices for topping.

Wash and trim the remaining soft fruit, then mix with the lemon juice and all but 6 tablespoons of the raspberry coulis.

Press the fruit into the lined moulds, top with one more piece of dipped bread, then weight between two plastic trays overnight.

Serve the puddings with the apple sorbet and the remaining coulis.

Individual Chocolate Soufflés

Serves 4

4 tablespoons caster sugar, plus extra for dusting
2 tablespoons plain flour
2 tablespoons Dutch cocoa powder, plus extra for dusting
1 tablespoon cold margarine
100ml / 4 fl oz soya milk
50g / 2 oz unsweetened chocolate, finely chopped
1 large egg yolk
2 large egg whites

Grease 4 shallow ramekin dishes (or any small ovenproof porcelain dish with straight sides) and dust them with caster sugar, shaking out the excess.

In a bowl, blend together half the caster sugar, the flour, the cocoa powder and the margarine until the mixture resembles breadcrumbs.

In a saucepan, bring the milk to a boil, then whisk in the sugar and cocoa mixture, together with the chocolate, and cook over a moderate heat, whisking continuously, for 1 minute or until the mixture has thickened. Allow to cool.

Preheat the oven to 200C / Gas 6.

In a bowl, lightly beat the egg yolk, then beat in the chocolate mixture.

In separate bowl, beat the egg whites until they hold soft peaks, then add the remaining sugar, a little at a time, continuing to beat the meringue until it holds stiff peaks. Stir a quarter of the meringue into the chocolate pastry cream to lighten it, then gently but thoroughly fold in the remaining meringue.

Divide the mixture between the prepared ramekins and bake for 12-15 minutes.

Dust with cocoa powder and serve immediately.

Opposite: Individual Chocolate Soufflé

Poached Red and White Pears with Vanilla and Cinnamon

Serves 4

8 very small pears
1 bottle red wine
1kg / 2¼ lb caster sugar
4 star anise
2 vanilla pods, split
4 cinnamon sticks
juice of 2 lemons
200ml / 7 fl oz crème anglaise (see page 136)
½ teaspoon ground cinnamon

Pour the wine into a large pan, add two cinnamon sticks, one vanilla pod, two star anise and half the caster sugar, bring to the boil and simmer for 5 minutes.

In a separate large pan, put 500ml / 16 fl oz water and the remaining caster sugar, cinnamon sticks, vanilla pods and star anise, plus all the lemon juice. Bring to the boil and simmer for 5 minutes.

Peel and core the pears – keep them whole and retain the stalks. Put four in each pan and simmer until just soft, about 10 minutes. Allow to cool. (The pears may be stored in the cooking liquid in the refrigerator for several days.)

Mix half the crème anglaise with the ground cinnamon.

Cut the white pears in half and make each half into a fan: place flat side down on a chopping board, and cut lengthwise into 15-20 fine slices without severing at the thin end, then press down and the pear will fan out.

Place the red pears upright on large white plates, with the white pears fanned on either the side.

Drizzle over the two crème anglaise sauces and serve.

❋ Garnish with a dusting of icing sugar, mint sprigs and redcurrants.

Pear Tarte Tatin with Vanilla Ice Cream

Serves 4

4 pears
250g / 8½ oz puff pastry
150g / 5½ oz caster sugar
2 tablespoons water
2 vanilla pods, split
1 x Vanilla Ice Cream recipe (see page 140)

Preheat the oven to 180C / Gas 4. Thinly roll out the pastry on a lightly-floured surface. Cut four 10cm / 4-inch circles.

Boil the sugar and water together for a few minutes until golden brown. Remove this caramel mixture from the heat and leave to cool for 5 minutes.

Place the sliced vanilla pods in four 10cm /4-inch tartlet tins. Pour the caramel on top. Peel and core the pears, and slice them in half. Fan each half into very fine slices. Place the curved side in the caramel. Cover with the puff pastry disc. Bake for 30 minutes, until crisp and golden.

To serve, turn the tarte tatin on to a plate so that the pastry is underneath. Serve warm or cold with ice cream.

❋ Chef's Tip

For a dessert treat, try this Banana Tarte Tatin. Follow the recipe for Pear Tarte Tatin, but use six firm bananas instead of the pears. Slice the bananas fairly thinly. I love to eat this with Bitter Chocolate Ice Cream (see page 140) – the sweetness of the bananas is beautifully offset by the bitter chocolate!

Opposite: Pear Tarte Tatin with Vanilla Ice Cream

134

Apple and Blackberry Crumble with Raspberry Coulis and Crème Anglaise and Vanilla Ice Cream in a Tuile Basket

Serves 4

A great English classic pud turned into a stunningly presented dessert and here adapted for the Jewish table by the use of a non-dairy ice cream so that it can be eaten as part of a meat meal. The combination of colours and textures come together beautifully to form a feast for the eyes.

FOR THE CRÈME ANGLAISE

400ml / 14 fl oz soya milk
75g / 2½ oz caster sugar
1 vanilla pod
8 egg yolks
200ml / 7 fl oz soya cream

To make the crème anglaise (pouring custard):
Simmer the soya milk with half the caster sugar and the vanilla pod. Whisk together the egg yolks and the remaining caster sugar until pale and fluffy. Pour the simmering soya milk into the yolk mixture, whisking continuously, then put back on the heat and cook gently, making sure it doesn't boil, until the custard coats the back of a spoon. Strain through a fine sieve and allow to cool.

≈

FOR THE RASPBERRY COULIS

100g / 3½ oz raspberries
25g / 1 oz icing sugar

To make the coulis, liquidise the raspberries with the icing sugar, then pass through a fine sieve.

4 Granny Smith apples, peeled and diced
200g / 7 oz caster sugar
100g / 3½ oz blackberries
100g / 3½ oz plain flour
60g / 2 oz margarine

≈

1 x Vanilla Ice Cream recipe (see page 140)
4 tuile baskets (see Plain Tuiles recipe, page 146)

Preheat the oven to 150C / Gas 3.

Put the apple into a pan with 100g / 3½ oz of the caster sugar and a little of the margarine, and cook gently until soft. Drain and mix in the blackberries.

Put the flour, along with 50g / 1¾ oz of margarine and 100g / 3½ oz of caster sugar in a food processor and pulse until the mixture resembles breadcrumbs.

Place four 10cm / 4-inch metal cutters on a baking sheet. Fill them with the warm apple and blackberry mixture, top with crumble, then bake in the oven for 20 minutes until the top is golden.

Put on plates, carefully remove the cutters, drizzle over the raspberry coulis and crème anglaise, and serve along with a scoop of ice cream in each tuile basket.

Warm Glazed Plum Tart with Vanilla Ice Cream

Serves 6

400g / 14 oz puff pastry
800g / 1¾ lb plums
55g / 2 oz caster sugar
1 x Vanilla Ice Cream recipe (see page 140)

≈

FOR THE CRÈME PATISSERIE
500ml / 16 fl oz soya milk
125g / 4½ oz caster sugar
1 vanilla pod, split and scraped out
75g / 3 oz plain flour
7 egg yolks

To make the crème patisserie, whisk the egg yolks with 125g / 4½ oz caster sugar, add the plain flour and whisk to a pale, thick consistency. Scrape the vanilla pod into the milk, then add whole pod. Bring the milk to the boil, pour on to the egg yolks and flour mixture, and whisk until blended. Return the mixture to the saucepan and set on a low heat. Whisk continually until you have a thick custard. Pour into a tray or bowl and cover with cling film to stop a skin forming. Let it cool down and take out the vanilla pod.

Preheat the oven to 200C / Gas 6.

Roll out the puff pastry thinly on a lightly-floured surface and use it to line a 22cm / 8½-inch flan tin. Allow to rest for 20 minutes, then bake blind for 20 minutes (see page 151). Increase the oven temperature to 250C / Gas 9.

Cut plums in half, stone them, sprinkle with 55g / 2 oz caster sugar. Place in a pan and cook for 5 minutes over a moderate heat to draw out some moisture, then drain well.

Spread a 1cm / ½-inch deep layer of crème patisserie over the bottom of the flan tin. Arrange the plums on top, then bake for 25 minutes. Serve with vanilla ice cream.

Bread and Butter Pudding with Honey Ice Cream

Serves 4

1 medium chola (sliced 5mm / 2 inches thick, crust on)
70g / 3 oz margarine, melted
200ml / 7 fl oz soya whipping cream
200ml / 7 fl oz soya milk
6 eggs
200g / 7 oz caster sugar
1 vanilla pod, split
pinch of salt
25g / 1 oz sultanas
100g / 4 oz apricot glaze (melted apricot jam)
icing sugar to dust

≈

FOR THE HONEY ICE CREAM
1 x Vanilla Ice Cream recipe (see page 140)
      with 50g / 2 oz of honey churned through the mixture
      while making the ice cream
1 tuile basket per serving (see page 146)

Mix milk, cream, eggs, sugar, salt and split vanilla pod. Leave to stand for 1 hour, then sieve. Grease an earthenware dish with margarine. Brush chola slices with melted margarine, then place in the dish in layers with slices slightly overlapping, sprinkling sultanas between each layer.

Add the custard mixture on top, making sure the bread absorbs the mixture. Place dish in a large roasting tray half-filled with hot water. Cook for 45 minutes at 170C / Gas 3. Remove from oven. Brush a thin coating of warmed apricot glaze over the top of the pudding.

To serve, place a ball of ice cream in a tuile basket on a large plate. Cut a 7cm / 3-inch square of pudding and place in the centre of the plate. Dust with icing sugar. Serve with raspberry coulis and crème anglaise (opposite).

137

Ice Cream and Sorbets

Opposite, from left: Strawberry Ice Cream, Bitter Chocolate Ice Cream, Mango Sorbet, Pistachio Ice Cream and Champagne Sorbet

Vanilla Ice Cream

Serves 6

500ml / 16 fl oz soya milk
100g / 3½ oz caster sugar
2 vanilla pods, split in half lengthways
6 egg yolks
150ml / 5 fl oz double cream substitute

Heat the milk, half the sugar and the vanilla pods in a pan and simmer for 2 minutes. Discard the vanilla.

Meanwhile, whisk together the yolks and remaining sugar until pale.

Pour the milk into the egg mixture, whisking continuously. Return to the heat and cook gently, stirring continuously, until it thickens slightly. Cool in a bowl of iced water.

When cold, stir in the cream and churn in an ice cream machine for 15 minutes until firm, then freeze.

❉ You can re-use the vanilla pods several times. Simply rinse them, wrap them in cling film and keep them in refrigerator.

Bitter Chocolate Ice Cream

Serves 6

500ml / 16 fl oz soya milk
100g / 3½ oz caster sugar
2 vanilla pods, split in half lengthways
6 egg yolks
150ml / 5 fl oz double cream substitute
100g / 3½ oz dark chocolate (70% cocoa solids), grated

Heat the milk, half the sugar and the vanilla pods in a pan and simmer for 2 minutes. Discard the vanilla.

Melt the chocolate in a glass bowl set over a pan of simmering water. (Alternatively, melt it in a Pyrex bowl in the microwave, heating it for 10 seconds at a time, stirring and repeating.)

Meanwhile, whisk together the yolks and remaining sugar until pale. Pour the milk onto the egg mixture, whisking continuously, until it thickens slightly.

Add the melted chocolate to this crème anglaise.

Cool in a bowl of iced water. When cold, stir in the cream and churn in an ice cream machine for 15 minutes until firm, then freeze.

Chocolate Chip Ice Cream

Serves 6

1 x Vanilla Ice Cream recipe (see above)
100g / 3½ oz dark chocolate (70% cocoa solids), grated

Follow the method given for vanilla ice cream, then, just before you finish churning, when the ice cream is almost firm enough to freeze, add the grated chocolate and churn for a further 2 minutes only. Freeze.

Banana Ice Cream

Serves 6

1 x Vanilla Ice Cream recipe (see above)
2 large ripe (but not brown) bananas

Follow the method given for vanilla ice cream. At the very last minute (to prevent it turning brown), dice the banana, add to the mixture in the ice cream machine, and churn a little, but do not mash the banana too much. Freeze.

Strawberry Ice Cream

Serves 6

1 x Vanilla Ice Cream recipe (see page 140)
200g / 7 oz strawberries
50g / 1¾ oz icing sugar

Chop half the strawberries into 5mm / ¼-inch dice.

Purée the remaining strawberries with the icing sugar and pass through a fine sieve.

Just before you finish churning the vanilla ice cream, add the diced strawberries and churn to break them down a little.

When you are ready to take the ice cream out of the machine, pour in the purée and churn a little to get a rippled effect. Freeze for an hour, then serve.

Pistachio Ice Cream

Serves 6

1 x Vanilla Ice Cream recipe (see page 140)
50g / 2 oz shelled pistachio nuts

Blanch the pistachio nuts by covering them with boiling water, cooking on 100% power for one minute in the microwave, or bubbling for the same time on top of the stove. Drain well, then slip off the skins. Finely chop the nuts and set them aside to dry on a plate.

Add the chopped pistachio nuts to the basic ice cream mixture before churning.

Honey and Cinnamon Ice Cream

Serves 6

500ml / 16 fl oz soya milk
50ml / 3 tablespoons runny honey
2 cinnamon sticks
6 egg yolks
50g / 1¾ oz caster sugar
150ml / 5 fl oz cream substitute

Heat the milk, honey and cinnamon sticks in a pan and simmer for 5 minutes. Remove from the heat and allow to infuse for 10 minutes.

Whisk together the egg yolks and caster sugar until pale.

Pour the milk onto the egg mixture, whisking continuously, then return to the pan and heat to 80C, so it is pasteurised. Cool in a bowl of iced water. When cold, add the cream and churn in an ice cream machine until firm. Freeze.

141

Sorbet Syrup

Makes 900ml / 1½ pints

450g / 1 lb caster sugar
400ml / 14 fl oz water
55g / 2 oz glucose

Place the ingredients in a pan and simmer for 3 minutes. Once cool, it can be kept almost indefinitely in a sealed jar in the refrigerator or dry store until you need it.

Mango Sorbet

Serves 6

142

12 ripe, but not bruised, mangoes, peeled and stoned
200ml / 7 fl oz sorbet syrup (see above)
juice of 2 lemons

Place the mango flesh with 100ml / 4 fl oz of the sorbet syrup and the lemon juice in a liquidiser, then blend until smooth. Pass through a coarse sieve.

Taste the mango purée and, if necessary, add more sorbet syrup and lemon juice – the amount will depend on the juice/acid in the mango, but bear in mind that sorbets lose a bit of sweetness on freezing.

Churn until firm in an ice cream machine, then freeze.

Raspberry Sorbet

Serves 6

8 x 100g / 3½ oz punnets of raspberries
400ml / 14 fl oz sorbet syrup (see above)
juice of 1 lemon

Place the raspberries in a liquidiser with 300ml / ½ pint of the sorbet syrup and the lemon juice and blend until smooth. Pass through a fine sieve.

Taste the raspberry purée and, if necessary, add more syrup, bearing in mind that sorbets lose a bit of sweetness on freezing.

Churn in an ice cream machine until firm, then freeze.

Lemon Sorbet

Serves 6

zest and juice of 7 large lemons
500ml / 16 fl oz sorbet syrup (see above)

Pour the sorbet syrup slowly into the lemon juice and zest, whisking continuously, until the balance of acidity and sweetness is about right – you will probably need about 400ml / 14 fl oz, but bear in mind that sorbets lose a bit of sweetness on freezing.

Churn in an ice cream machine until firm, then freeze.

Passion Fruit Sorbet

Serves 6

4 passion fruit
300ml / ½ pint sorbet syrup (see page 142)
juice of a lemon

Cut the passion fruit in half, scoop out the seeds, flesh and juice, and discard the hard skin. Mix the passion fruit with the sorbet syrup.

Taste and, if necessary, add some lemon juice, but bear in mind that sorbets lose a bit of sweetness on freezing.

Churn in an ice cream machine until firm, then freeze.

Champagne Sorbet

Serves 6

750ml / 27 fl oz Champagne
300ml / ½ pint sorbet syrup (see page 142)
juice of a lemon

Mix the Champagne and lemon juice with the sorbet syrup.

Churn in an ice cream machine until firm, then freeze.

Lime Sorbet

Serves 6

zest and juice of 10 very large firm limes
500ml / 16 fl oz sorbet syrup (see page 142)

Gradually pour the sorbet syrup into the lime juice and zest, whisking continuously.

Churn in an ice cream machine until firm, then freeze.

✳ If you prefer a more mellow taste, you can first simmer together the syrup, juice and zest for 5 minutes.

Pink Grapefruit Sorbet

Serves 6

143

zest and juice of 7 pink grapefruit
500ml / 16 fl oz sorbet syrup (see page 142)

Gradually pour the sorbet syrup into the grapefruit juice and zest, whisking continuously, until you have the balance of acidity and sweetness you require, but bear in mind that sorbets lose a bit of sweetness on freezing.

Churn in an ice cream machine until firm, then freeze.

Carole Sobell's

Petit Fours

Plain Tuiles

Serves 6

100g / 3½ oz icing sugar
100g / 3½ oz egg whites
100g / 3½ oz softened margarine
100g / 3½ oz plain flour

Preheat the oven to 220C / Gas 7.

Mix together all the ingredients until smooth.

To make tuiles for petit fours, first make a circular stencil. You can do this by cutting a circle out of a tupperware lid or old ice cream container, with a 5cm / 2-inch circular hole in the middle of it.

Place the stencil on a non-stick baking sheet, spread the tuile mixture over it with a palette knife, then carefully lift it off, leaving behind a little round disc *(top right)*.

Repeat until the baking sheet is covered with discs.

Bake for 6 minutes or until the edges turn golden.

Whilst still warm, lift the tuile biscuits from the tray *(centre right)* and lay them in a tuile tray *(bottom right)*. Alternatively, shape them over a rolling pin, if making petit fours, or over a small glass or cup if making tuile baskets.

✳ The basic mixture can be stored in the refrigerator for several days, then used for different recipes below.

146

Opposite: Plain Tuiles

Chocolate Tuiles

Serves 6

100g / 3½ oz softened margarine
100g / 3½ oz icing sugar
100g / 3½ oz egg whites
50g / 1¾ oz plain flour
50g / 1¾ oz unsweetened cocoa powder

Follow the method on page 146.

Orange Tuiles

Serves 6

100g / 3½ oz softened margarine
100g / 3½ oz icing sugar
100g / 3½ oz egg white
115g / 4 oz plain flour
zest of 3 oranges
50ml / 2 fl oz orange juice

Follow the method on page 146.

Coconut Tuiles

Serves 6

100g / 3½ oz softened margarine
100g / 3½ oz icing sugar
100g / 3½ oz egg white
100g / 3½ oz plain flour
50ml / 2 fl oz coconut milk
75g / 2½ oz toasted desiccated coconut

Follow the method on page 146.

✳ Chef's Tip

*Here Carole uses a tuile tray to shape her tuiles,
but you can easily do it by shaping them
round a rolling pin or a glass*

Mini Chocolate Ices on Sticks

Serves 6

1 x Vanilla Ice Cream recipe (see page 140)
300g / 10½ oz dark chocolate (70% cocoa solids)

Ball the ice cream with a melon baller and re-freeze for an hour.

Melt the chocolate in a glass bowl set over a pan of simmering water. (Alternatively, melt it in a Pyrex bowl in the microwave, heating it for 10 seconds at a time, stirring and repeating.)

Insert a cocktail stick into a ball of ice cream, dip it in the chocolate, then re-freeze.

Passion Fruit Sorbet Dipped in Chocolate

Serves 6

1 x Passion Fruit Sorbet recipe (see page 143)
300g / 10½ oz dark chocolate (70% cocoa solids)

Ball the passion fruit sorbet using a melon baller, then re-freeze for 3 hours.

Melt the chocolate in a glass bowl set over a pan of simmering water. (Alternatively, melt it in a Pyrex bowl in the microwave, heating it for 10 seconds at a time, stirring and repeating.)

Insert a cocktail stick into a ball, dip it in the chocolate, and re-freeze until ready to serve.

Hazelnut Clusters

Serves 6

200g / 7 oz hazelnuts
250g / 8½ oz caster sugar

Preheat the oven to 190C / Gas 5. Blanch the hazelnuts by covering them with boiling water and bubbling for a minute on top of the stove. Drain well, then slip off the skins. Roast the nuts in the oven for 15 minutes until golden.

Put the sugar in a heavy-based pan with 50ml / 2 fl oz water and heat until it has dissolved and caramelised.

Stir the hazelnuts into the caramel and spread out on an oiled baking tray. When cool enough to touch, take four caramel-covered hazelnuts and shape into a pyramid. Repeat until all hazelnuts are used.

Allow to cool completely, then store in an airtight tin.

149

Cape Gooseberries Dipped in Caramel

Serves 6

150g / 5½ oz cape gooseberries
250g / 8½ oz caster sugar
50ml water

Put the sugar in a heavy-based pan with 50ml / 2 fl oz water and heat until it has dissolved and caramelised.

Peel back the outer leaves and dip the fruits in the caramel. Make sure you don't get caramel on your fingers – it's hot. Leave to cool on a plate.

❋ The dipped fruit will only last 8 hours.

150

NEW JEWISH CUISINE

Brandy Snaps

Serves 6

125g / 4½ oz margarine, melted
175g / 7oz caster sugar
125g / 4½ oz golden syrup
125g / 4½ oz plain flour
1 teaspoon brandy
a pinch of ground ginger

Preheat the oven to 190C / Gas 5.

Place all the ingredients in a food processor and blend until smooth. Roll into small marble-sized balls, place on a baking sheet, and flatten slightly with the back of a spoon.

Bake for 8-10 minutes until they are golden brown – they will now look flat and perforated.

Allow to cool slightly, then mould over a rolling pin, if making petit fours, or over a small glass, if making baskets for ice cream.

Strawberry Tartlets

Makes 4

FOR THE PASTRY
200g / 8 oz soft plain flour
50g / 2 oz caster sugar
a pinch of salt
125g / 5 oz margarine, cut into pieces
1 egg yolk
15ml / 1 tablepoon soya milk
≈
100ml / 4 fl oz crème anglaise (see page 118)
100g / 3½ oz strawberries, thinly sliced

Make the pastry by putting the flour, margarine, salt and sugar into a food processor, then pulse until it resembles breadcrumbs. Add the egg and milk and pulse once more until a dough has formed. Wrap in cling film and allow to rest for 2 hours.

Preheat the oven to 220C / Gas 7. Roll out the pastry on a lightly-floured surface and use to line four 4cm / 1½-inch tartlet cases. Bake blind for 20 minutes (see Chef's Tip).

Just before serving – and no more than 4 hours beforehand – fill the pastry cases with the crème anglaise and top with the strawberries.

151

✳ Chef's Tip

Baking blind means cooking the pastry on its own. Put the pastry in a lightly-greased dish according to recipe. Line the pastry case with greaseproof paper, weight it with baking beans or dried raw pulses, and bake until three-quarters done, or according to recipe.

Opposite, clockwise from left: Truffles, Cape Gooseberry Dipped in Caramel, Tuiles, Brandy Snap, Hazelnut Cluster, Strawberry Tartlet

Palmiers

Serves 20

250g / 8½ oz puff pastry
100g / 3½ oz icing sugar
1 teaspoon cinnamon

Roll out the pastry on a lightly-floured surface to a thickness of about 3mm / ⅛ inch, and roughly 35cm / 14 inches square.

Dust with the icing sugar and cinnamon, then roll up like a Swiss roll and chill for an hour.

Preheat the oven to 230C / Gas 8.

Trim the ends of the roll, slice into discs 3mm / ⅛ inch thick, place them flat on a greased baking tray, and bake for 6-10 minutes.

Dust with icing sugar before serving. Eat the same day they are cooked.

152

Honey Madeleines

Serves 20

Deliciously sweet, soft-textured petit fours for when you really want an impressive round-off to a special occasion meal. You could even serve them at a cocktail party as a sweet canapé. Easy to make, they also store well in an airtight container for up to three days.

2 eggs
75g / 2½ oz caster sugar
10g / ¼ oz soft brown sugar
85g / 3 oz plain flour
1 teaspoon baking powder
85g / 3 oz margarine, melted
10g / ¼ oz runny honey

You will need a madeleine tray for this recipe – you can buy one at any cook shop.

Beat the egg and sugars together until pale in colour.

Sift together the flour and baking powder, and fold into the egg mixture.

Stir in the melted margarine and honey, then allow to rest in the refrigerator for an hour.

Preheat the oven to 230C / Gas 8.

Lightly grease a madeleine tray, then dust with flour. Spoon in the mixture and bake for 5 minutes.

Leave to cool.

❋ Chef's Tip

For a soft-centred surprise, place a raspberry in the centre of each mould before baking.

Chocolate Truffles

Serves 6

300g / 10½ oz chocolate (70% cocoa solids)
150g / 5½ oz margarine, melted
100ml / 4 fl oz cream substitute
50ml / 3 tablespoons alcohol, such as brandy, rum or
*   crème de menthe*
cocoa powder for dusting
icing sugar for dusting

Melt the chocolate in a glass bowl set over a pan of simmering water. (Alternatively, melt it in a Pyrex bowl in the microwave, heating it for 10 seconds at a time, stirring and repeating.)

Whisk the cream into the melted margarine, add the alcohol, then whisk into the melted chocolate.

Chill. When set, shape into balls using a small melon baller. Roll in cocoa powder then dust with icing sugar, and refrigerate until ready to serve.

Coconut Truffles

Serves 6

300g / 10½ oz chocolate (70% cocoa solids)
100ml / 4 fl oz coconut milk
150g / 5½ oz margarine, melted
50ml / 3 tablespoons coconut rum liqueur such as Malibu
50g / 1¾ oz desiccated coconut

Melt the chocolate in a glass bowl set over a pan of simmering water. (Alternatively, melt it in a Pyrex bowl in the microwave, heating it for 10 seconds at a time, stirring and repeating.)

Melt the margarine in a pan or in the microwave. Whisk in the coconut milk, add the Malibu, then whisk this into the melted chocolate. Chill in the refrigerator.

Lightly toast the coconut on a baking sheet under a hot grill for a few seconds.

When the truffle mixture is set, shape it into balls using a small melon baller, and roll in desiccated coconut.

Refrigerate until ready to serve.

153

Orange Truffles

Serves 6

500g / 1 lb 2 oz chocolate
100ml / 4 fl oz cream substitute
150g / 5½ oz margarine, melted
50ml / 3 tablespoons Grand Marnier
zest of 2 oranges

Melt 300g / 10½ oz of the chocolate in a glass bowl set over a pan of simmering water. (Alternatively, melt it in a Pyrex bowl in the microwave, heating it for 10 seconds at a time, stirring and repeating.) Melt the remaining chocolate in a separate bowl.

Melt the margarine in a pan or in the microwave. Whisk in the cream, add the Grand Marnier and orange zest, then whisk the cream mixture into the larger amount of melted chocolate. Chill in the refrigerator.

When set, shape into balls using a small melon baller, dip in the second bowl of melted chocolate, and refrigerate until ready to serve.

Hazelnut Truffles

Serves 6

300g / 10½ oz chocolate
100ml / 4 fl oz cream substitute
150g / 5½ oz margarine, melted
50ml / 3 tablespoons rum
200g / 7 oz hazelnuts, finely chopped

Melt the chocolate in a glass bowl set over a pan of simmering water. (Alternatively, melt it in a Pyrex bowl in the microwave, heating it for 10 seconds at a time, stirring and repeating.)

Melt the margarine in a pan or in the microwave. Whisk in the cream, add the rum and half the hazelnuts, then whisk into the melted chocolate. Chill in the refrigerator.

When set, shape into balls using a small melon baller, roll in the remaining hazelnuts, and refrigerate until ready to serve.

154

Opposite: Assorted truffles

Carole Sobell's
Entertaining

Eating in has become one of the great 'nights out',

whether it's with family and friends for a special occasion

or just as a way of relaxing at home.

The formal dinner party has given way to a

more casual style of entertaining at home, but

getting it right still depends on careful planning...

A feast for the eyes

First impressions count for a lot – and that's as true of food as it is of people. Get the look right and you're halfway to creating a culianary sensation. In this section we take a look at a number of different scenarios for entertaining at home, with a suggested menu for each kind of party, along with some tips for ensuring that you create the right atmosphere and a meal to remember. The recipes are all taken from this book, and you're bound to find many other dishes which work equally well together. Just choose the combination to suit the occasion and your tastes, and enjoy putting together something special for your family and friends.

Today, whether you're throwing a dinner party for a few friends or inviting the mob over for Sunday lunch, there's a vast array of cuisines and recipes you could offer them. But while food fashions may come and go – traditional salmon is replaced with seared tuna, while black forest gateau gives way to bitter chocolate tart – the basic ingredients of successful entertaining remain the same.

As a caterer and party planner, I'm happy to entertain anything from a small dinner party to a banquet with a thousand guests. It's taken for granted that the food will be good – I hope! – but it's setting the scene, creating the right mood and paying attention to detail, that turns the occasion into something memorable … and it's exactly the same if you're entertaining at home.

Here are a few guidelines to help you plan your home entertaining. Combined with a selection of tried and tested recipes from the pages of *New Jewish Cuisine*, I trust it will ensure that the hosts enjoy their evening as much as their guests!

The guests

Food has always been at the heart of a Jewish home, from the traditional Friday night dinner to special festivals for family and relatives. But entertaining at home is no longer just for these occasions – it's also an opportunity to bring together friends from a wider circle, with differing tastes and cultural influences.

It is important to consider the mix of people and what sort of conversation and atmosphere you are likely to get when you add them together! You should also think about how many you can comfortably accommodate, depending on the occasion. For example, around six to eight should be right for a dinner party where you want to keep everyone involved in the conversation. If it's 'pop round for drinks' before going out, you may like to invite many more – but if that means standing room only, take care not to let it go on too long.

Make sure all your guests

Carole Sobell's

· Menu ·

Tartare of Smoked Salmon

RECIPE ON PAGE 51

Roast Rack of Lamb with Pommes Anna

RECIPE ON PAGE 109

Chocolate Truffle Heart with Summer Berry Fruits

RECIPE ON PAGE 118

≈

The Romantic Dinner for Two

Scene-setting is essential if you're planning a romantic rendezvous for two, but you also want to spend your time with your partner, and not in the kitchen. So greet your special someone with well-chilled champagne, enjoy a delicious dinner that you've prepared in advance, finish with an irresistible dessert – and leave the dishes until the morning! Much of the work can be done in advance in this menu, so once you've dressed the table you'll have bags of time to dress for dinner. It offers a delicious salmon starter, ready to place at the table before taking your seats, and an impressive main course. Vegetables can be blanched earlier in the evening, then simply refreshed in hot water before serving. The lamb can be prepared and sealed ready to pop into a hot oven. To keep the romantic theme, the rack of lamb can be cut in half and arranged in a heart shape on the plate. And it's all rounded off – of course – with a chocolate heart.

know who else has been invited and try to give them a few background details such as shared interests to help break the ice. Give them an idea of what to expect – whether it's going to be snacks with drinks, a light supper, or a full three-course dinner.

It's important to make an effort to meet individual tastes and diets. Do all your guests keep kosher? Is anyone allergic to nuts? Any vegetarians? Or does some awkward soul simply hate a particular ingredient?

If your invitation includes children, make sure you have catered for their needs and tastes too. If you have young children of your own but it's adult-only time you're after, then make sure they have their own entertainment sorted out – or that you've allowed plenty of time for them to be safely tucked up in bed before your guests arrive.

Once you've got your guest list sorted out, better start getting ready for the show…

Some dishes definitely need to be prepared in advance!
Try your hand at this spectacular dessert on page 128

It may be tempting to offer the same old favourites so you don't have the worry of offering your guests something you've never cooked before. But what a shame to miss out on an opportunity to surprise your family and friends with something new and interesting, particularly if it's a special occasion. So, once you've chosen your dishes, practise them first. Then look at how much you could prepare in advance and freeze, chill or store until the big event.

Finally, plan to have a back-up at the ready for that precisely-timed hot soufflé which someone just could not resist taking a peek at for you! A refreshing fruit salad and good ice cream, nicely presented, is easy to prepare in advance and will still provide a perfect finish to your meal.

Much of the table presentation can also be done in advance – here are a few suggestions to add to your dinner party check-list:

❋ Make sure you have matching polished cutlery and glassware

❋ Hand-polish plates – and make sure your hands are not wet when handling the edges to avoid fingerprints

❋ Choose co-ordinating, well-pressed table linen

❋ A cold starter can be pre-set on the table

❋ For a special party, sprinkle glitter on the tablecloth for added sparkle

❋ Dessert plates can be decorated in advance if you have enough room to lay them out.

Preparation

Good planning will take a lot of the hard work out of entertaining at home – and it should leave stress-free hosts able to enjoy the meal with their guests.

Give yourself plenty of time to plan your menu and work out a schedule for the evening to make sure all your dishes come together at the right time, to avoid a last-minute panic.

160

The Traditional Sunday Lunch

• Menu •

Cream of Vegetable Soup
with Garlic Croûtons

or

Crown of Melon with a
Cascade of Berry Fruits

RECIPES ON PAGES 37 AND 42

Traditional Roast Beef
and Yorkshire Pudding
and Seasonal Vegetables

RECIPE ON PAGE 115

Apple and Blackberry Crumble
with Raspberry Coulis and
Crème Anglaise and
Vanilla Ice Cream
in a Tuile Basket

RECIPE ON PAGE 136

≈

Few people can resist an invitation to Sunday lunch, but if the host is to enjoy the day as much as the guests, the first rule is: Start early! This menu, with a choice of starters and desserts, should suit most families. Much can be prepared in advance – the soup can be frozen – but don't make fruit salad before the day, and pep it up with fresh orange juice just before serving. The individual crumbles can be made as one large dessert, if you prefer. When it comes to roast beef, I find the best kosher cut is ball of the rib – a little expensive but well worth it. Ask your butcher for a piece that's well-hung, so it's tender. Don't skimp on the joint – allow a 4-5 lb joint for a family of six. Any left-overs can always be served as cold cuts the next day, though I doubt you'll have much left!

Scene-setting

Giving some thought to the kind of atmosphere you want to create for your guests will really enhance the occasion. Think about the style of food you have chosen to serve and how you would like it to look on the plate and at the table – then create an appropriate setting with your choice of tableware and decorations, lighting and music. Don't forget, the food is only half the occasion; the scene you set will transform a meal into a memorable event.

Here are a few scene-setting tips to remember:
✳ Organise some cool background music, but not too loud
✳ Dress the table with flowers, candles, or garden foliage
✳ Plan the lighting to ensure a warm atmosphere – candles add a soft glow to a dinner party and should be lit before guests go to sit at the table. Scented candles can add to the atmosphere, but make sure they are not too strong or they'll be over-powering
✳ For more formal events, use name cards at each setting. Try something eye-catching and unusual – a gold pen to write on a leaf from the garden, for example
✳ Serve coffee in the lounge if possible to allow your guests to relax away from the dining table.

Bring on the food!

It doesn't matter whether it's a lavish dinner or a simple bowl of salad, when it comes to serving your food, presentation is the key. Set out to impress – and satisfy your guests by feeding their eyes first.

Here's how to make your meal a real show-stopper:
✳ Use large presentation dishes that will display your food at its best
✳ Depending on the dish, dust the plate with paprika, icing sugar or cocoa powder
✳ To add colour and dimension, garnish the plate with fresh herbs, or use a banana leaf on the base of the plate and serve the food on top

✳ Don't be tempted to pile too much on the plate. Instead, carefully place potatoes and vegetables round meat or fish to really enhance the presentation
✳ For an imaginative way to serve canapés, cover pieces of wood with remnants of material or use slate tiles or even spare floor tiles which have been varnished
✳ If you're serving nibbles with drinks, make sure they are an easy-to-handle one-bite size
✳ Always have white wine very well chilled and serve it in sparklingly clean and polished glasses
✳ Make sure you have still or sparkling water on offer. Add a twist of lime or lemon to water glasses and if you have no room to chill the water, then add ice cubes to the glasses. Look out for an attractive bottled water in a coloured glass which you could match to your table décor.

Finally, remember that, whatever you serve to your guests, aim to feast their eyes first so that they will enjoy the meal from the first glimpse to the last mouthful. I love serving canapés because of the opportunity it gives me to really surprise and delight people with a particularly delicious little treat, and I love desserts for the same reason.

That attention to detail, and the desire to serve beautiful food, have strongly influenced the recipes offered in this book. I hope you find them as much fun as I do!

Carole Sobell's

· Menu ·

Smoked Salmon Rosettes

RECIPE ON PAGE 18

Fish and Chips

RECIPE ON PAGE 26

Thai Chicken Satay

RECIPE ON PAGE 25

Mini Potato Latkes

RECIPE ON PAGE 31

Thai Fish Cakes

RECIPE ON PAGE 29

Petit Fours

VARIOUS RECIPES ON PAGES 146-154

Cape Gooseberries in Caramel

RECIPE ON PAGE 149

Dark chocolate mints

≈

The Drinks Party

163

If you're catering for a crowd, or simply want to relax with friends, then canapés are the answer. It's one of my favourite ways of entertaining because you can create some fabulous treats and they look great. But "popping round for nibbles" shouldn't mean that anyone goes home hungry! Start with cold canapés, so you have something to offer people straight away. Smoked salmon is a good appetiser to get the taste buds ready for a variety of cold and hot treats. Use your imagination to think of fresh ways to serve your canapés. Brighten up the tray with a few flower heads, a night light or a handful of berry fruits. When the party includes children, it's fun to serve canapés which are miniature favourite meals like mini burgers, and fish and chips in paper cones. End with a selection of petit fours – any dessert in the book can be served in mini form – and then I like to serve Bendicks mints with coffee.

The Celebration Dinner

There are times when you want to make an extra effort to mark an important anniversary, a family gathering or other special occasion – and what better way than to treat your guests to a fine dinner?

Make sure you can offer something special to everyone, including a choice of dishes to tempt all tastes and preferences, perhaps a fish dish or an interesting vegetarian course. Prepare as much as possible in advance so that you can join in the celebrations too. In the menu shown here, even the potato rosti can be made ahead of time then finished off to a hot and perfectly crisp dish at the last moment. For the noisettes of lamb, allow a generous four slices per person – you should get around one-and-a-half portions per loin of lamb.

When it comes to rounding off a special occasion meal, it has to be a soufflé – it's a spectacular dessert which is

164

· **Menu** ·

Wild Mushroom Soup
Garnished with Chopped Chives

RECIPE ON PAGE 36

―――――

Noisettes of Lamb with
Potato and Parsnip Rosti
with a Panache of Vegetables

RECIPES ON PAGES 106 AND 107

―――――

Individual Chocolate Soufflés
with Crème Anglaise
and Seasonal Berry Fruits

RECIPES ON PAGES 132 AND 136

bound to impress, and it's not as difficult as you might imagine once you're not afraid of it. I've always had a sweet tooth, and I used to love surprising friends who popped round by offering them a coffee and a soufflé to finish off an evening. You should, however, practise it first before serving it at an important celebration – but as long as your soufflé rises to the occasion, so will you!

✻ Style Tip

Candles bring a glow to any dinner table – even if you don't have an elaborate candelabra like this exotic arrangement!

Index

167

168

✳ Final Tip

*If all else fails –
call Carole Sobell!*

Carole Sobell Ltd, Unit C, 2-10 Carlisle Road, London NW9 0HN. Tel: 020 8200 8111
Kuperard, 311 Ballards Lane, London N12 8LY. Tel: 020 8446 2440. publications@kuperard.co.uk